DATE DUE

#47-0108 Peel Off Pressure Sensitive

---♦ ♦ ♦---

"A practical, easy to read book. After reading it, I had a stack of notes and a new to-do list that I've already started work on."

James Alexy
President and CEO
Sealy, Inc.

"Terrific and readable! If you want to understand the tone, temper and quality of high performing organizations and how they get that way, run to your local bookstore. You won't be disappointed."

Warren Bennis
Distinguished Professor of Business
School of Business,
University of Southern California
Author of *On Becoming a Leader*

"Witty and important. People who need to deceive themselves will hate this book. Everybody else will love it."

Albert J. Bernstein
Co-author of *Dinosaur Brains*

"Very useful and hardhitting: shifts the focus of strategy to fact-based action and provides a roadmap for ensuring implementation of strategic intentions."

James I. Cash, Jr.
James E. Robinson Professor of
Business Administration
Harvard Business School

"A book of great impact without hype, fancy pictures, or silly jargon—vital reading for any top executive struggling with managing the challenges in the new Europe."

Johan H. W. Christofferson
Director
S. J. Warburg Securities, London

"Shapiro has put her touch and our attention on a critical and often overlooked aspect of management: the ways in which the unexamined assumptions of corporate managers shape their behavior and the futures of their firms. If you have ever found yourself voicing such assumptions as 'We know how to win in our business' or 'The facts are obvious' or 'Of course we know what our product is,' you should buy this book and think twice."

James Clawson
Professor, Organizational Behavior
The Darden School
University of Virginia

"A fascinating and important book. No manager can afford not to read and re-read it. The lessons it provides are absolutely fundamental to individual and corporate success. She has managed that rarest of feats—writing a management book that is readable, practical, and profound."

Allan R. Cohen
Co-author of *Managing for Excellence*
and *Influence Without Authority*

"At the bottom, this is a book about managerial courage. Shapiro points out skillfully and convincingly how consensus, so routinely sought and feigned, is the death knell of any organization. 'Dissent,' she writes, 'is often the ultimate act of allegiance.' Hooray for a book that teaches us how to link hands while facing the music."

Allan Cox
Author of *Straight Talk for Monday Morning* and *The Achiever's Profile*

How Corporate Truths
Become Competitive Traps

How Corporate Truths Become Competitive Traps

How to keep the things that
"everyone knows are true"
from becoming roadblocks to success

—————————— ✦ ✦ ✦ ——————————

Eileen C. Shapiro

John Wiley & Sons, Inc.

New York • Chichester • Brisbane • Toronto • Singapore

In recognition of the importance of preserving what has been written, it is a policy of John Wiley & Sons, Inc., to have books of enduring value published in the United States printed on acid-free paper, and we exert our best efforts to that end.

Copyright © 1991 by Eileen C. Shapiro

Published by John Wiley & Sons, Inc.

All rights reserved. Published simlutaneously in Canada.

Library of Congress Cataloging-in-Publication Data

Shapiro, Eileen C.
    How corporate truths become competitive traps / by Eileen C. Shapiro.
      p.   cm.
    Includes index.
    ISBN 0-471-51643-0
    1. Management. 2. Organizational effectiveness. 3. Strategic planning. 4. Competition. I. Title.
HD31.S432   1991
658.4'012—dc20   90-23149

Printed in the United States of America

91 92 10 9 8 7 6 5 4 3 2 1

To Ben

CONTENTS

──────────────◆ ◆ ◆──────────────

to the market inside your company. If you don't understand it, both you and your employees lose.

"The executive art is nine-tenths inducing those who have authority to use it in taking pertinent action." Every person in an organization makes at least a hundred decisions a day. When enough of these decisions are wrong, they can overwhelm even the most elegant strategy.

PREFACE

———————————— ✦ ✦ ✦ ————————————

My impetus for writing this book was my observation of what I call "the mysterious equation:" Despite the combination of smart managers, clear incentives to win, the latest in managerial techniques, and large investments in internal reports and consultants' recommendations, the effort to improve performance often results in little or no real change.

Why does this happen? In my experience, the root cause is deceptively simple: when the "truths" held within organizations are incorrect, they lead to a pattern of poor decisions that cannot be corrected until the "truths" themselves are corrected. In theory, addressing this problem is easy; the key is "organizational learning," which allows current assumptions to be modified and thereby creates the willingness for change. In practice, however, learning of this sort requires critical review and challenge, and few people are able to sincerely challenge what they already "know" to be true.

What is needed to break the hold of the mysterious equation, in my view, is not more theories, or more techniques, or more reports; there are plenty of these already. The fundamental requirement is instead the ability to recognize when a corporate truth has become a competitive trap.

For this reason, this book focuses on the eight generic assumptions that, though seemingly obvious, are most frequently incorrect and cause the most harm to companies. It is a book of my observations, and uses examples to illustrate the competitive traps discussed, rather than to prove their existence or to explore the particular companies in depth. My hope is that you will enjoy this book—and that it will encourage you to think about the corporate truths in your company in a new way.

Eileen C. Shapiro
The Hillcrest Group, Inc.
Cambridge, Massachusetts

INTRODUCTION

--- ✦ ✦ ✦ ---

What Competitive Traps?

It's not what we don't know that gives us trouble, it's what we know that ain't so.

—WILL ROGERS

Will Rogers was right: It's not what you know that can hurt you; it's what you know that ain't so. For those who run companies, this adage is particularly important; often, the biggest risk is not your competitors, but your own "corporate truths." Misguided by incorrect assumptions, even very capable managers may persistently make what appear to be bizarre mistakes and poor decisions. Consider a small sample of the evidence:

• • •

Everyone knows that the Datsun 240 Z is a great made-in-Japan, sold-in-America success story. But not everyone knows that at the end of 1969 the first Z rolled off the boat with the name . . . *Fair Lady.*

How did this happen? It wasn't for lack of information. Datsun's Yutaka Katayama, a Japanese national stationed in California, repeatedly told his superiors in Tokyo that the company's new sports car needed a powerful name, like Lion or Tiger. Yet headquarters held firm to its belief that Americans wanted cars with English names like Cedric or Bluebonnet—or Fair Lady.

That the Z went on to be a great success is a testament to Katayama's ingenuity: he physically pried the Fair Lady nameplates off and replaced them with the only name that could save the car without getting him fired—240 Z, the company's internal designation for the car.

Katayama had a long record of success as his company's U.S. representative. Short of using his screwdriver, why couldn't he convince his superiors in Tokyo about the realities of the U.S. market?

• • •

In 1982, amidst industry-wide losses totaling more than $3 billion, U.S. Steel Corporation chairman David Roderick made the following pronouncement: "We

3

have been shocked out of our complacency and smugness. We now realize that American industry has no manifest destiny to be always first, always right, always best.''

Should Roderick have been shocked? Hardly. Since the 1950s, the possibility of future problems had been clear: Foreign producers were rapidly adding new capacity; demand growth in the United States was slowing. Nonetheless, the U.S. steel companies collectively increased their capacity by 40 million tons. And while the new foreign mills were being equipped with state-of-the-art technology, the U.S. steelmakers continued to invest in the older technology of open hearth furnaces. The new foreign mills could take advantage of the easy-to-mine and lower-cost iron ores from Australia and Brazil; U.S. mills used lower-quality, higher-cost ores from North American mines in which they held equity interests.

Despite the impending threat, the big integrated steel producers in the U.S. acted as though they still set the rules. Each partially upgraded all its various mills rather than overhauling a few completely. As a result, the typical American mill was a mixed bag of both world-class and antiquated equipment. The companies also accepted labor agreements that increased the costs of shutting down noncompetitive facilities. The result? When closures could no longer be avoided, good equipment had to be idled with the bad, with shutdown costs for some mills of close to $1 billion. The foreign competition had acted predictably; the final blows came from actions taken by the domestic producers themselves.

• • •

The Swimsuit Manufacturers' Association, known in the industry as SWIM, was puzzled. Despite several seasons of high-fashion designs, sales were below expectations. In 1987, SWIM conducted some basic market research to find out why.

The research painted a simple picture. Most women did not have the figures for the sexy and revealing suits that were being shipped to the retailers. So although many potential buyers were trying the suits on in the stores, four out of five were walking out without making a purchase. A fiber supplier to the industry offered this explanation: "I say that most women would rather have a root canal without novocaine than buy a swimsuit."

Why was the research even needed? After all, even a stroll through a mall or along a beach should have told the swimsuit manufacturers much of what they needed to know.

• • •

A few years before Northwest Airlines fell prey to raiders and the resulting 1989 purchase of the company by Alfred Checchi, Northwest's management approached Fallon McElligott, a leading Minneapolis ad agency, about some advertising work. Since service quality was a possible platform for the new campaign, Pat Fallon, Fallon McElligott's chairman, listened to the airline's passengers as he developed his ideas.

He became increasingly concerned about what he heard. "Northworst," as some passengers had begun to call it, appeared to be falling far short of its claims. "We found the service wasn't nearly as good" as described by Northwest management, Fallon says. But when he made his report to Steven G. Rothmeier, then chairman of the parent company of Northwest Airlines, "Steve asked us to redo the work based on Northwest's perception of its own product."

Rothmeier claims that Fallon McElligott misunderstood the airline's on-time reports. But even if Rothmeier was correct, the reports were irrelevant if the customers were dissatisfied (as was likely the case, since the airline had one of the highest rankings of airline passenger complaints for most of 1987 and part of 1988). Why wasn't the company interested in new facts?

• • •

A bus line in Great Britain that received complaints of its drivers speeding past waiting passengers gave this formal response: "It is impossible for drivers to keep their timetable if they have to stop for passengers."

How could the passengers ever have become secondary to the schedule?

• • •

These cases illustrate the effects of corporate truths that have become competitive traps. The problem is especially tricky because these traps tend to be invisible: implicit assumptions are, by their nature, rarely questioned—they're just considered part of the givens of the world.

What first got me thinking about corporate truths was my experience with a company I'll call Amalgamated Industries, a well-run multi-billion dollar organization with strong managers. The company had an enviable track record, with one important exception: it was losing share and margins in markets with slow growth and experienced customers. Yet while common sense says that businesses need to be managed differently when industry growth slows, these businesses were being managed as though demand had not slowed at all.

THE PROBLEM AT
AMALGAMATED'S SPIES DIVISION

Take Amalgamated's Special Purpose Integrated Electronic Systems division (SPIES), which designed, assembled, sold, and serviced highly specialized research equipment. The division president, Kenneth Coombs, had built SPIES from a $35 million afterthought into a $650 million business, based on a technological breakthrough that he had managed about a decade earlier.

But the markets that SPIES served were changing. The pace of innovation had slowed, and demand shifted to lower-priced and less complex systems. Even in the premium segments, the buyers had become highly concerned about price. And in all segments, sales were moving from naive first-time buyers to sophisticated replacement buyers.

Despite this new environment, SPIES' top management continued to submit budgets based on aggressive sales targets, with heavy investments in advanced research and other overheads designed to allow the division to respond quickly to the anticipated growth in the market. They were not alone; the other Amalgamated divisions that participated in markets with similar dynamics also submitted "hockey stick budgets," in which "next year" was always going to be the first year of sustained growth and profitability, despite the flat trend in the previous years.

So why did SPIES and other Amalgamated managers persist in making decisions that had so little chance for success in the marketplace? Here is the perspective of Alex Sarris, general manager for a product line within the SPIES division.

Alex Sarris's Story

"What you have to understand about an Amalgamated manager is that the goal is recognition. That's how you move up the ladder. And that recognition comes from the size of the revenues you control and whether they are growing—nothing else is nearly as important. A business without growth is not good, regardless of whether you can make the business profitable. Even if you are in a flat market and you take out costs, you are told, 'I know you can take costs out, but what I really want is to see this thing grow.'

"When I first came to SPIES, I worked for Ken [Coombs], and I could see that the same game wasn't going to keep working for us. There was going to be a crash. I would talk to him about the need for multiple price points and investments in improved reliability and service, and about what the competitors were doing. But Ken didn't want to spend a lot of time thinking about customers and competitors because his model of the world told him that these things didn't affect revenues.

"See, Ken had a 'tape' that played in his head, and it said that if we could just make another technological breakthrough like ten years ago, everything would be rosy again. He knew we needed to grow, so he would push the numbers up and tell the sales guys to make up the difference. But when the sales guys would say that they couldn't meet the numbers, the tech guys would say, 'but we have all these great products.' Then whenever we got into trouble, Ken would cut the service and sales budgets. R&D was sacred— it never got touched.

"Of course it didn't work, and eventually Rob Diller was brought in to replace Ken. Rob's 'tape' was discipline. He had come in from another division that had been losing $5 million a year and he had gotten it to breakeven. So when he looked at our division, he saw a big operation that was sloppy, and he did what he had been brought in to do: pull out the costs and keep the businesses growing. But he didn't understand the need to invest in reliability and service either, and he set the same kind of growth targets that Ken had.

"The product line I ran was strategically very important to the division, but it was in a flat market with little potential for a technological breakthrough. But even though I got the costs out and increased our share while upping our prices, I wasn't in the winners' circle because I wasn't in a product line with dramatic growth rates. For example, when we presented our budgets, the other product lines got two hours to make their presentations. I got ten minutes. I'd get an 'atta boy' but all the body language was 'who gives a hoot?' Growth, even growth at the expense of profits, was the most important thing, because as an Amalgamated general manager, you are expected to grow your business and you are expected to grow it like crazy.

"I could have lied and been a hero—you know, set high growth targets even if they didn't make sense and then do any crazy thing to meet them. That's the way most of the others played the game. When Tom Jakes [manager of one of the other product lines] got promoted, he committed to big numbers I knew he couldn't meet because the growth wasn't going to be there. He was considered a big hero—at first. But of course he couldn't deliver on his commitments. He was relegated to the dinosaur heap—oh, I'd say about a year and a half after he was promoted.

"Then there was this thing called 'team playing.' When I tried to explain to Rob that the market was flat, I was accused of not being a team player, see? When I told him about the service problem, I wasn't a team player either. He didn't want to hear the truth—he just wanted everyone to say, 'Yes sir!'

9

"So Tom probably did the smart thing when he committed to those numbers. It's easier to take the chance that you can bring off 'mission impossible'—something may change, you may get transferred, who knows what may happen. But when you watch a colleague getting crucified for submitting a low-growth budget, you know that it's better to commit to the numbers than to try to run the business the way you would if it were your own."

FIGURING OUT THE REAL PROBLEM

The traditional way to look at the problem at Amalgamated is to conclude that since the managers were consistently making the wrong decisions, the "obvious" solution would be to replace them, tighten the management control systems, increase the penalties for failure, or implement the old standby— changing the organizational structure of the company.

A closer look, however, revealed that most of these "obvious" fixes were already in place. The managers were capable of and deeply committed to winning; the reporting systems were proven and rigorous; and the need for getting close to the customer was accepted. In addition, the managers understood that there was little mercy for those who "missed their numbers." In their view, the price of not meeting their commitments was sure and swift: the end of career advancement, sharply reduced discretion, social ostracism, and eventual termination from the company.

What hadn't happened, however, was a fundamental change in the implicit assumptions about the "right way" to run these businesses. The business unit managers knew how to manage for growth and thought they were in growth environments; the executives at corporate wanted growth in revenues and rewarded those managers who met this goal. The result was that the business unit managers kept submitting unrealistic growth budgets and corporate kept approving them.

Since my work with Amalgamated, I have seen the power of incorrect assumptions to lead managers into poor decisions, despite heavy investment in the latest in management techniques, analytic tools, and consultants' reports. Based on the last ten years of such observations, I have come to the conclusion that what typically sets companies careening down the wrong path in the first place is not some missing managerial technique, but rather misplaced confidence in one or more of the following eight core assumptions:

1. We act on the facts.

2. We know what the facts are.

3. We have all the facts we need.

4. We know how to win in our business.

5. Of course we know what our product is.

6. We know how to make a buck.

7. We understand what our people want.

8. Our people know what to do.

That a poor assumption will cause major trouble may seem obvious; few managers would knowingly make decisions based on faulty assumptions in any of these areas. Yet unwitting adherence to incorrect assumptions is precisely what had happened in each of the examples cited earlier. At Amalgamated's SPIES division, for instance, almost all of the eight were misaligned with reality to some degree, from the rewards given by corporate (emphasis on revenue growth rather than profits), to the understanding of what customers wanted (emphasis on more bells and whistles rather than better service and lower price), to the ability to use critical information (emphasis on team playing rather than listening to uncomfortable data).

These eight core assumptions form the backbone of this book. Each chapter explores one of the eight, showing why the assumption is often wrong and how to alter the mental "tape" that keeps erroneous ideas and perceptions playing repeatedly, with the same predictable results. As you read each chapter, challenge your own assumptions about why your company is successful, what your customers want, how your competitors operate, and other key issues. If you're like most people, you may learn some surprising things about your own tape. Though it is human nature (and a necessary expediency) to develop patterns of thinking and behaving rather than creating the world anew each moment, in the rapidly changing world of business, these patterns can become staid or inappropriate. When this happens, the assumptions themselves become the greatest obstacle confronting the organization. Or in the immortal words of Walt Kelly's comic-strip character Pogo:

"We have met the enemy and he is us."

CHAPTER ONE

◆ ◆ ◆

We Act on the Facts

Anyone who says businessmen deal in facts, not fiction, has never read old five-year projections.

—MALCOLM FORBES

THE ASSUMPTION:

We act on the facts.

THE REALITY:

Gut instincts usually win,
even when they're wrong.

THE RESULT:

"Business as usual" even though the world is
changing and despite announcements of
bold change and new initiatives.

SOME COMMON SIGNS WHEN
GUT FEEL IS IN CONTROL

- Change that violates the old rules of thumb is rarely considered, much less implemented.

- Endless debate about the facts almost always prevents modification of how things are done today.

- New initiatives get great press but usually are only partially implemented at best.

- Good ideas get just about to the point of commercialization before they somehow are torpedoed from within the organization.

- Despite frenzied activity, there are certain beliefs or "sacred cows" that are off-limits for discussion or change.

- Some obvious strategic options are never really considered.

- Old habits reassert themselves as soon as the crisis is over.

- The few new ideas that are accepted seem to lose impact because competitors get there faster.

- Some parts of the organization seem to be insulated from new corporate rules that mandate change.

- It seems like more time is spent rationalizing deteriorating performance than acting to improve the situation.

Imagine a company whose line employees don't set to work in earnest until after morning tea at ten o'clock, labor at their jobs until noon, lunch until two, and then work for another two and a half hours, at which point they have afternoon tea and call it a day. Paperwork is done with pens and blotting paper, as it has been for centuries. Visitors are ushered into the building by red-frocked doormen known as "waiters," in homage to the company's origins in a seventeenth-century coffeehouse.

This isn't a scene from a Victorian novel; rather, it's business as usual at Lloyd's of London, as described by brokers who deal with the company's underwriters. Quaint? Most certainly. Viable at the end of the twentieth century? Only with great difficulty. And not surprisingly, competitors with more efficient ways of doing business are moving into areas in which Lloyd's was once without peer. During the 1980s, for example, the company's share of the £2.8 billion marine insurance market in London, which accounts for policies on half the world's ships, fell from 66 percent to 50 percent against such rivals as the Institute of London Underwriters, an association of more than a hundred international insurance companies.

CORPORATE TUGS-OF-WAR

Getting bogged down in convention and "the way we do things around here" happens in organizations regardless of their age or industry. At Lloyd's, the obvious trappings and touches of tradition just make the problem more apparent. But even in companies whose entrepreneurially minded leaders and employees work inhumanly long hours to succeed and whose operational systems reflect state-of-the-art technologies, faithfulness to old rules of thumb often creates obstacles.

For example, how many times have you noticed organizations that:

17

- Continue to throw massive amounts of resources into basic research when the technologies have become mature? (Think about Ken Coombs at Amalgamated's SPIES division. It's hard to find a high-tech company that isn't following Coombs's strategy.)

- Ignore market research on the premise that their products are so good "they will sell themselves"? (A classic example is Kevlar, a duPont product that has five times the strength of steel but by 1987 had racked up an estimated $200 million in losses. The marketing manager for Kevlar summed up the problem this way: "Kevlar was the answer, but we didn't know for what.")

- Think they know what the customer *should* want and proceed on that basis? (In the 1980s, women planning business trips were courted by a variety of special products, such as "Lady Hilton" rooms, a "Traveling Woman" program from Ramada, and even a booklet with tips on packing and safety from Westin. Today all three programs have been disbanded. Comments one analyst: "Finally someone got the bright idea to ask businesswomen just what it was they were looking for. And wonder of wonders, it turns out what they really want is a good hotel.")

- Design products for what the designers or management—rather than the company's potential customers—would like to buy? (This may be why Swissair initially installed its internally designed Skydreamer seats in its first-class cabins instead of the industry-standard Slumberettes. Within three months, on the basis of the complaints it received, the airline decided to retrofit all of its planes.)

- Develop marketing plans targeted at the kind of people they would like to be their market rather than those

18

who actually are? (Remember what happened to the swimsuit manufacturers that kept their eyes on the customers they preferred instead of the ones who, although less glamorous, made up the bulk of the market.)

- Assume that no one could produce a product that matches theirs in quality but sells for less and therefore don't worry about competitors? (How else can you explain the Xerox engineer who, after hearing a speech about customer complaints, declared that the machine's maintenance rating was "as good as or better than the competition out there, and I can't help it if the customer doesn't like it"?)

- Think of selling as a matter of relationship-building when their customers now buy almost exclusively on price and delivery terms? (Through the 1970s and into the 1980s, many executives of U.S. steel companies were still out on the golf course with their customers when their new competitors were beating them on price and quality.)

In all likelihood, you've observed similar situations in companies that you work for, buy from, or supply. And you've probably wondered how the organizations in question could possibly *not* have been able to come to grips with the hard facts in a timely way. The answer is that in the battle between gut feel and hard facts, gut feel usually wins, even when it no longer matches the requirements for success.

Of course, few management teams would acknowledge that *they* operate on the basis of anything other than the facts. In reality, however, managers facing the need for change often fall into one or more of the following behaviors: *apparent paralysis*, in which management seems incapable of making the tough decisions; *deceptive activity*, in which many decisions are made, but few if any truly challenge outmoded instincts; and *quiet reversal*, in which previously made tough decisions somehow become undone over time.

Apparent Paralysis

On the surface, inability to make the hard decisions may seem to be a lack of movement. In fact, however, the lack of a new decision is really a vote for the status quo; the organization does move, but primarily in the direction dictated by the decision rules from the old strategy.

Take the case of a company we'll call Juniper Technologies, a leading U.S. manufacturer of advanced medical equipment. A high flyer for its first twenty years, the company had slowly lost market share during the previous decade. But because the total market continued to grow, Juniper's sales had increased as well. When the overall market stopped growing, though, the evidence of Juniper's declining share could no longer be ignored, and the company set out to reclaim its turf.

That's also when the internal battles began. On the one hand, the company's market research indicated significant potential for a simplified product line designed for use in smaller hospitals and outpatient clinics, code-named the "Juniper Junior." On the other hand, the idea of a stripped-down product neither appealed to Juniper's executives nor fit their experience as to how to win new customers. In short, Juniper's managers wanted growth but they didn't want the Junior.

Stuck between the market research data and their gut feel, top managers at Juniper experienced a paralysis of sorts, incapable of either approving the Junior or aborting the project. Worse, they became mired in all manners of delay: endless discussions and meetings, continual revisions of the reports and recalculations of the numbers, pointless arguments, and more and more market research—even though the results kept pointing to the same conclusion. One ex-Juniper employee, a lead engineer on the Junior development team with almost a quarter century of tenure at the company, gave his perspective on what had happened and why.

"Listen, for the last twenty years, we had evidence that a 'Juniper Junior' would expand our market. But it's really been the past ten years or so that it's been a real issue, because we've been losing share. That's when we got serious about investigating the possibilities.

"The reason that it's taken so long is that Bob [the CEO] and most of the rest of top management never really believed in their guts that there was a mass of potential customers for the Junior. It wasn't a matter of the facts. How many times did we talk to the customers? We spent a ton of money on market research. It was that they just didn't *believe* what the customers were saying. And I'll tell you why. We wanted to make the perfect product. And to us that meant with all the bells and whistles. It wasn't that we didn't understand the theory of market segmentation. It was that thinking about segments required us to put ourselves into other people's heads and think about what *they* wanted instead of what *we* wanted.

"And that's what we couldn't do. People who are analytically trained, the way Juniper people are, think they make their decisions based on data, but often they really are making them at the gut level without understanding that that's what they're doing. So what I think happened was that neither Bob nor most of the other top guys could make sense of the data because in their guts the data didn't feel right. The result was a battle between the data and their guts. And as long as the battle went on, they couldn't make decisions—and the more data they got, the more the battle was prolonged. They couldn't kill the project because of

21

all the data that supported it, and they couldn't act on it either because it felt wrong."

At last sighting, Juniper had just undertaken another study on the feasibility of the Junior. Or as the ex-Juniper engineer noted: "Working at Juniper is like being in a soap opera—you come back a year later and it doesn't take long to figure out that nothing much has changed."

Juniper's paralysis occurred early in the game and was precipitated by the need to consider a different kind of product. In other cases, the paralysis sets in at the last—but critical—moment. Consider the case of Xerox, which set out to diversify from copiers into products that would create "the office of the future." The company did in fact meet its goals, inventing the personal computer three years before Apple Computer even incorporated (and eleven years before the introduction of the Macintosh). Unwilling to institute all the changes in corporate policies and structure that would have been required to market the device, however, Xerox let the opportunity evaporate. Here's what happened in a nutshell:

- In 1970, Peter McColough, appointed only two years before as the new chairman of Xerox, announced his goal of "establishing leadership in what we call 'the architecture of information.' " In the same year, the company established the Palo Alto Research Center, known internally as PARC, to develop the products to create the new architecture.

- By 1973, PARC's researchers had invented most of what could rightfully be called a user-friendly personal computer: the first "mouse," the first command protocol that used icons, the first truly easy word-processing program, the first local-area communications network, the first object-oriented programming language, and the first laser printer.

22

- In 1976, the same year that Wang showed its first word processor, Xerox vetoed the idea of taking the new system, now called the Alto, to the market either as a word processor or as a more general computer workstation.

- In late 1978, frustrated by myriad internal obstacles that made commercialization nearly impossible, the Alto team put forth a plan for manufacturing and marketing Xerox's personal computer system. Three months later, at the end of January 1979, the following response was received: "We have concluded that Xerox will not pursue the proposal you have prescribed; however, we appreciate the thought you have given to the many issues covered in your proposal." With these words, Xerox's ability to commercialize the Alto effectively was killed, despite McColough's continuing reiteration of his goals and despite the continuing deterioration of the company's copier business, which experienced a drop in share from 65 percent in 1977 to 49 percent in 1979.

At Juniper, the company couldn't even get started on meeting its goals; at Xerox, it couldn't continue beyond a critical point. At both, dependence on old priorities crippled the companies' abilities to capitalize on new opportunities. The result was mixed messages internally and lost opportunities in the marketplace.

Deceptive Activity

In other companies, what appears to be dramatic change is actually a smoke screen for the avoidance of decisions that run counter to long-entrenched habits and instincts. In these cases, the organization sincerely advertises its plan to become more efficient, more customer-focused, or more entrepreneurial, only to create a "new" company that is virtually indistinguishable from the old one.

Consider the differences between General Motors and Ford Motor Company as they both tried to regain domestic market share during the 1980s. Of the two, GM's approach, masterminded by Roger Smith, was decidedly the more dramatic. Stepping up to the chairmanship in 1981, Smith laid out a bold vision and took a number of sweeping actions aimed at the U.S. market. Key among these were the following:

- The company's first corporate reorganization since the 1930s

- Investment of more than $40 billion in its plants and equipment, much of it for robots and automation

- Acquisition of two technologically oriented companies, Electronic Data Systems and Hughes Aircraft

- Entry into a joint manufacturing venture with Toyota

- Creation of the Saturn Corporation, a pilot company within General Motors dedicated to producing U.S.-developed and -built cars that would be "import fighters."

Despite all these actions, however, from 1980 to 1989 GM's domestic market share slid from about 46 percent to less than 35 percent, while Ford's grew from about 17 percent to just over 22 percent. And even with its smaller revenue base, by 1986 Ford's total profits exceeded those of its larger rival.

What accounts for this difference in results? Part appears to have been due to the degree to which the two companies truly broke from their old ways of doing business. For example, Ford's $5 billion investment in the Ford Taurus and the Mercury Sable was the result of Ford chairman Phillip Caldwell's conclusion that the company had lost the confidence of the

American consumer and that nothing short of a wholesale revolution on the product side would regain it. From this conclusion came the truly tough decision: to change everything about the way the company designed and manufactured cars. Or as Caldwell described it afterward: "We committed ourselves to the design, manufacture, and sale of superb products, with no excuses. They were to be *drivers'* cars—functional, comfortable, good-looking, and distinctive."

Some of GM's goals may have sounded similar. But consider the reaction of Saturn's top manager, Richard G. LeFauve, as a reporter read the following description to him: "All-new aluminum engine, fail-safe sophisticated marketing research and highly automated assembly technique . . . a revolutionary change from a company and industry that heretofore stressed slow, evolutionary change." LeFauve smiled and nodded in agreement as he listened to what sounded like a description of a 1990 Saturn. The only problem was, as the reporter quickly pointed out, that it came from a *1979* book (*On a Clear Day You Can See GM*) and was part of an earlier GM press release describing the *1970* Vega. Twenty years later, under LeFauve's leadership, Saturn may finally provide a way for GM to live up to its claims.

The decisions taken by GM management made great copy for press releases and magazine articles. But many of these decisions simply reinforced old assumptions about how to manage the business, only with greater fanfare and more money than before. GM's starting point assumed that the company already knew how to deliver what the customers wanted; Ford's assumed that the company did not. The result was that Ford's investment had a faster payback because it focused squarely on a central issue: designing and building cars that customers wanted to buy.

Quiet Reversal

The third way the status quo prevails over the facts occurs when a company is unable to stick to the hard decisions that must be made on a repeated basis. That was the problem confronting the Chrysler Corporation in 1989 when, having achieved a stunning, almost miraculous comeback in the early 1980s, the company was again facing very serious problems. In part the cause of this return to the brink was that the cost consciousness so vigilantly pursued during Chrysler's first turnaround had been only a temporary measure. Said one middle manager: "There was this feeling that we should let people enjoy some of the fruits of the three or four [years of austerity]. Some enjoyed them too much."

Enjoying the fruits of austerity should not have meant abandoning three or four years of discipline. Yet in some cases, Chrysler reverted to old, unrestrained ways of spending. Product planning at Chrysler was one area that apparently lost sight of the company's cost-consciousness goals, resulting in massive and very expensive duplication: The $33,000 Chrysler TC was introduced as a luxury convertible but was perceived, in one industry analyst's words, as a "dead ringer" for the $15,000 Chrysler LeBaron convertible. Similarly, the $25,500 Chrysler Imperial was seen as almost indistinguishable from the $21,000 Chrysler Fifth Avenue—and from three other company models that sold for as much as $12,500 less. As a result of product-planning mistakes like these, Chrysler had to eliminate 18 models in a period of two years—more models than Ford's entire product line at the time.

As Chrysler and countless other companies have discovered, old habits die hard because they feel right and are comfortable. The risk is that over time these feelings of rightness and comfort allow the old decision rules to reemerge, overwhelming the new behaviors that have been initiated.

When What Feels Right Hurts Performance

Gut instincts like the ones that drove the decisions of the companies in the preceding examples originate from diverse sources. In some cases, they are manifestations of business habits founded on past successes. Such habits, according to Akio Morita, chairman of Sony Corporation, caused the U.S. radio manufacturer that developed the first transistor radio in the 1950s to elect not to produce it. Unable to change its focus from the large, tabletop models that had always fueled its success, this company effectively stepped aside, allowing its new Japanese competitor to develop a worldwide market for "Sony transistor radios."

In other cases, the gut feel that guides managers is really a philosophical position, based on beliefs about what is right and wrong and therefore about how a business *should* be run or what a customer *should* want. Beliefs like these reportedly led Control Data Corporation to invest nearly a billion dollars in a computer-based education product, called Plato, without ever recovering its costs. The investment was justified on the basis of social need rather than market viability. Perhaps not surprisingly, the company's founder, William C. Norris, shunned market research on the product. "All we'd do is uncover all the problems," he explained. "We'd never go into it."

And finally, gut feel can be nothing more than the personal likes and dislikes of key managers. Inventor/managers like Henry Kloss, for example, entrepreneur extraordinaire of stereo and television equipment, typically love to innovate. But they sometimes lose their companies when the effort has to shift from inventing to managing cash flow, as happened to Kloss at Advent Corporation. Similar gut reactions frequently underlie the decisions of managers who tackle the tasks they excel at and enjoy with gusto, but shun those activities at which they are less adept.

Whatever their sources, however, the resulting instincts can make it difficult for managers to accept or act on counterintuitive data, even when these instincts have become decoupled from the new requirements for success. The upshot in these cases is the inability to create momentum for a new direction, no matter how compelling the evidence or how apparent the need. When this happens to companies like Juniper, Xerox, General Motors, and Chrysler, the victory of gut feel over hard facts is often obscured by the battle. The ex-Juniper employee sums up the situation this way: "At least in a real tug-of-war, you got your red shirts and your blue shirts, and if a guy in a red shirt goes to the blue side, you can see what he's doing. But in this game, you can't see who is where. It's as though there's a fog over the whole game."

Cutting through this fog requires managers to assess how willing they are to make and stick to decisions that go against the accumulated tradition and habits of an organization. Two actions can aid in this process. The first is to make a conscious choice between sticking with the old ways and making the changes indicated by the facts. The second is to understand the potential gut-level blocks to these decisions, to make sure that management can live with them—or to find managers who can.

FACING THE TRADE-OFFS

Managers like those at Juniper must make choices when they discover that their gut reactions do not match the needs of all their target markets: They can either incur the opportunity costs of sticking to the way they know and like to do business, or they can change. Of the two, sticking to the old ways is usually far easier but often requires a trade-off between current comfort and potential performance.

When Sticking to Gut Feel is the Best Answer

In many instances, companies may elect to remain faithful to their traditions and to pay the price of doing so. But in other cases, sticking to the old ways of doing things requires less sacrifice than might at first appear, because the company's bottom-line performance really will be better if they continue to follow the old rules. Management at a company we'll call Rhone River Products, a diversified chemical products company, discovered this when it considered ways to generate incremental revenues.

The sales force at Rhone River was one of the company's most important assets. Deeply committed to serving the customer, the salespeople would censure a colleague who took more than an hour to return a customer's call, almost regardless of the reason for the delay. As a result of this dedication to customer service, Rhone River had steadily increased its share and earned price premiums in several industrial product categories that its competitors considered low-tech commodities, deserving of little or no customer attention.

Amidst these successes, however, Rhone River experienced some glaring failures. One major flop was GL-10, an updated version of a popular product, GL-9. The main difference between the two was that GL-10, while similar in appearance and price to the product it replaced, had been designed to lower performance standards, reducing product costs.

But the product didn't sell. Or, more accurately, the sales reps didn't sell the product. Obsessed with serving the customer, these reps did not see the new product as able to pass *their* standards because it was not an improvement over the older product in terms of either price or performance.

Should Rhone River have pursued additional products with a similar profile to GL-10? Probably not. GL-10 had not been an important part of the company's strategy. Developed almost as an afterthought, it was one of those products intended to generate a little extra revenue at minimal cost. When it became apparent that products like GL-10 would not only require more than an incremental effort but might also jeopardize one of the company's most important strengths, its sales force, the decision not to target future GL-10s was fairly straightforward. In this case, the trade-off between the status quo and change was clearly weighted on the side of the former because Rhone River's regular product line still met the needs of the company's customers.

When Gut Feel Becomes a Religion

As management at Rhone River discovered, the cultural values that grow out of a company's tradition can take on the strength of a religion. When this happens, the question is whether the religion furthers the goals of the organization or has become an end in itself. Consider a few examples:

- An executive in a Japanese company that prides itself on cost control wants to incur a trivial expense to keep a key customer happy. The response: "Organization is more important than customer." The needs of one customer were subordinate to consistency in the way the company did business.

- Amana, a leading high-end kitchen appliance maker with the motto "Whatever you make, make it the best it can be," has the opportunity for tapping a vastly expanded market by using the company's brand name and manufacturing power to go after the low end of the microwave oven market. George Foerstner, Amana's founder, turns the idea down. He is uninterested, he says, in a product to be sold by "a part-time clerk in a lumber yard, or a tire salesman, or a temporary clerk at K mart."

- Cummins Engine, a manufacturer of heavy-duty diesel engines, enters 1990 fighting for survival. But though the company has been aggressive in lowering its costs, there are still some things it refuses to do: reduce its charitable spending, which ranks in the top 95 of the Fortune 500; reduce its R&D budget, which exceeds $100 million per year; or move from Columbus, Ohio, which is dependent on Cummins, despite the city's high labor costs and unionized work force. Says Cummins's chairman Henry B. Schacht: "Some say the company's main goal should be to maximize shareholder wealth. . . . I say no." His goal instead is "being fair and honest and doing what is right even when it is not to our immediate benefit."

■ No layoffs was a tradition at Digital Equipment Company. And layoffs were about the last thing that Digital management had to worry about during the company's dramatic climb from its 1957 founding to its position as the world's second-largest computer maker 30 years later. By 1989, however, growth had slowed and Digital's work force was too large—some say by as much as 50 percent. Rather than institute layoffs at that time, the company began to shift people, thousands of them, from both the factory floor and the corporate offices, into the sales force. One customer comments: "Our people cringe when they see a Digital salesman coming. Some don't know their own products. . . . Digital's hardware sells itself, which is a good thing because no one else seems to be."

Each of these companies faced the same question that Juniper's managers avoided: whether to stick to tradition and accept the costs of doing so. One can argue whether such strategies are sustainable—for example, Digital eventually announced layoffs—or even about whether they are correct. But by making a *conscious* decision, each company at least avoids the kind of interminable tug-of-war that incapacitated

Juniper, wasting the time and sapping the morale of the company's best people.

TESTING THE DECISION

Managers who understand their own gut reactions operate at a real advantage. Their awareness allows them to anticipate if they will be able to live with the consequences of their decisions, or whether their gut reactions will block the new direction they think they want to set. Those who opt for tradition can therefore confront whether they will be willing to forego certain incremental revenues and/or profits. Based on the data they had, for example, Juniper's managers could not expect both to regain share and to compete without a product like the Junior. Similarly, those who decide to go against tradition can assess whether they really will be willing to stick to their decisions over the long haul.

In some cases, of course, managers have no ethical choice but to change because the costs of maintaining the status quo are just too high, or because the adherence to tradition no longer serves any constructive purpose. Some managers in this situation nonetheless try to avoid the required change, citing "corporate culture" as their alibi. But as anthropologist Lionel Tiger argues, the difference between companies that have five layers of management and those that have twenty-two is managerial competence. In these cases, the defense of corporate culture needs to be recognized for what it is: a tired excuse for not making the tough decisions.

"What If" It Were You

Fortunately, it's possible to test such tough decisions in advance. But instead of asking the standard textbook questions

32

about strategy, what you in fact need to ask are questions that make the decisions real for you. Consider a few "what ifs":

- **What if** a company like Juniper decides to stay with its traditional market strategy and foregoes the opportunity presented by the Junior? How are you going to feel when you have to explain to the analysts on Wall Street that the company is no longer growing? How are you going to explain it to the people in your work force, who now will have little chance for promotion?

- **What if** a company like Cummins pictures itself as a leaner and meaner competitor than it has been in the past? Are you willing to shut down plants to achieve this goal? What if a community will endure real hardship if its main employer leaves town? How will you explain the situation to the people you see in church on Sunday? How will your children explain it to their friends and teachers at school?

- **What if** a company like Amalgamated Industries, described in the introduction to this book, requires a valued and faithful employee like Kenneth Coombs to shift from rocket scientist to marketing maven, and he can't make the transition? Are you going to replace him or keep him as head of the division? And if you replace him, are you going to find him another job elsewhere in the company or ask him to leave? What's it going to be like when you explain your decision to him?

- **What if** the new direction you have selected doesn't fit with research and development projects that have been long under way, or with major investments in plant and equipment that have just been completed? When Jan Carlzon took over Scandinavian Airlines Systems, for example, he immediately mothballed four

33

new Airbuses, for which the company had just paid $120 million, in favor of the continuing use of SAS's old DC-9s. His reasoning: business travelers, SAS's new target market, like frequent flights with no stops. Airbuses are cost-efficient only when fully loaded, which would have required SAS to schedule fewer daily flights, each with intermediate stops. Mothballing the new Airbuses was, in Carlzon's words, "the decision that made the most sense," because as tough as it was, it was the only one that fit the strategy.

Could you accept all the consequences of decisions like these—and then still make more decisions like them, year after year? When Colby H. Chandler took over as chairman of Eastman Kodak, he reorganized the company, forced decision making down deeper into the organization, and demanded—and got—shorter product-development cycles. But by 1989, the company was undergoing its fourth cost restructuring since the first one Chandler undertook in 1984. Should Chandler have shrunk Kodak's size earlier in one radical restructuring, as some of his critics suggest? "There is not a family in Rochester that isn't touched by Kodak in some way," Chandler notes. "How big a change can you make without destroying everything in the process?"

Taking the Gut Tests

In order to determine which options you are truly prepared to live with, it helps to develop a tangible picture about the potential decisions and their corresponding implications. Questions that elicit visceral responses are a simple and direct way of doing this:

- What will life be like in this firm if we decide to move in this new direction?

34

- What are the key decisions we are going to have to make over the next two to five years?

- How am I going to feel when I make these changes?

- Who will be angry with me?

- How will my job change?

- What am I going to have to give up that I really am going to miss?

- What am I going to have to do that I'm not going to like doing, that I'm not used to doing, or that is going to distress me deeply?

- What kind of company will we be after these decisions—and will I be proud to be part of it?

Gut questions like these should focus on the decisions that would be most dissimilar to today's actions and most uncomfortable for today's managers. Even the task of finding the right gut questions is, by its nature, an uncomfortable one. But so are the decisions themselves. Only by asking and honestly answering tough questions can managers hope to stick with tough decisions that break from instinct and tradition. If you ask the question and feel as if you couldn't live with the answer, you have to assess whether you've made the right decision—or whether you're the right person for the kind of decisions that are required.

Up Close and Personal

Making and sticking to the decisions required by an organization's new direction is tough enough, but often managers are also confronted with decisions that mean real personal sacrifices. The likelihood of finding yourself in this situation increases when you ask others to change, for they will look first to see whether those above them are willing to do the same. If they don't see sufficient evidence, they are likely to view the demands on them as unfair and hypocritical and will therefore resist the changes as much as they can. The gut question is this: If you ask others to change, will you be willing to share the pain?

When organizational change requires personal sacrifice, the first reaction is typically that the request is unfair. And sometimes, the request is never seen as fair, even when it seems more than reasonable to those outside the company. At Amtrak, for example, workers used to earn a day's pay for every hundred miles traveled. By those rules, they could earn four and a half days' pay for just under eight hours' work when they worked round-trip on the speedy Metroliner between New York City and Washington, D.C. Not surprisingly, since the rules have been changed to provide a week's wages for every forty hours worked, many still view the change as unjust. Complained one worker, who now works twenty days a month, compared with ten previously: "Everything I worked for has been taken away."

Similarly, many in management understand their own perquisites to be part of the compensation packages that they have earned over years of hard work. They may also justify such perks as essential to the satisfactory completion of their jobs. But often these same perks are major obstacles to achieving real change within the organization.

Imagine the following situation: The managers of an ailing company have completed a careful financial and strategic analysis. They have seen what must be done, communicated the message of mandatory austerity and sacrifice to the rest of the organization, and backed up their words with appropriate actions. Two months later, they begin a program of renovation and reconstruction of their personal offices, spending hundreds of thousands of dollars. Or they purchase new office furniture for themselves and leave their old furniture—which is still better than anyone else's in the company—on the curb for the trash collectors. Or they troop off for a planning meeting at a lavish resort a thousand miles away from the office.

The business press is full of such stories, and most veterans of organizations tell similar tales that they have observed first-hand. Unfortunately, nothing undermines the effort to embark on a new course more than indications that the top ranks are insulated from the sacrifices involved. Consider the internal reaction that greeted Merrill Lynch's decision to downsize for the 1990s and become a leaner and more efficient company. Having announced that it would terminate 3,500 to 4,000 people, the brokerage firm ordered the remaining employees to learn, in the words of one executive, to "treat the [firm's] money they spend as if it were their own."

The problem was real enough. At Merrill, as at other investment banks, expense spending almost came to be regarded as just another part of a lucrative compensation package. Michael Lewis, for example, ex-bond salesman and author of *Liar's Poker,* describes some of the excesses he observed at Salomon Brothers: firm limos sent to pick up friends, firm telephone charge cards lent to people outside the firm, firm limos used for weekend shopping sprees. Or consider the champion expense abuser, the person in Salomon's mortgage finance department who, according to Lewis, "put through enough phony expense reports from fictitious trips to buy himself a Saab with the proceeds."

Despite the apparent need at Merrill Lynch to rein in excess spending, however, by some accounts the company's campaign for change got off to a poor start. Employees, speaking anonymously to *The New York Times,* called top management's goal hypocritical, and recounted the perquisites offered to those at the top: Game hunts in India, dove hunts in Mexico, and fishing expeditions in Iceland, all intended for senior executives and big clients; in addition to trips to Paris for board members and their spouses; and the general opulence of everyday life for the company's senior executives.

Are such management perks required for Merrill's success? From the perspective of those lower in the organization, top management was simply refusing to practice what it preached. Former Merrill Lynch chairman Donald Regan agreed: "They got too used to limousines and perks. Look at the new headquarters. Mahogany paneling everywhere. The swish dining rooms. The chauffeured cars. See you in Boca Raton. See you at the Louvre. That attitude has permeated Merrill as well as the rest of Wall Street." But current management disagreed. Said president and COO Daniel P. Tully: "It's so small in terms of people's thinking—to pick on a trip or attack the use of a helicopter. I hope God will give them a larger perspective and less of a jealous streak."

Jealous streaks aside, however, it's difficult to get others to accept the negative aspects of change when those at the top aren't willing to as well, at least to some extent. Consider two success stories: Lee Iacocca took a $1 compensation package the year that he asked the rest of Chrysler Corporation to give back part of their compensation. The managers of Weirton Steel gave up their corporate country club, company-owned housing, reserved parking places, and executive dining rooms and took the same cut in compensation as everyone else in the company when they and the mill's unionized workers bought the facility from its previous owner, National Steel. In both organizations, the success that followed these actions probably would have been impossible had top management not signaled that everyone in the company was in it together.

In short, in situations that require sacrifices from other people, the really tough decisions often aren't those involving layoffs or telling others to change their habits; the really tough decisions are the ones that require the managers themselves to take a swig of the same medicine they have prescribed for the rest of the organization. And as for all such decisions, if the answer to gut questions that probe the tough issues is a resounding "NO WAY!," you need to reconsider if you are truly willing to act on the facts. If the answer is a reluctant "yes," then you've at least got a shot at making the indicated change.

• • •

Even though outdated gut reactions usually seem much more reliable and are certainly more comfortable than new data, their dangerous allure can be overcome. Think about Nissan Motor Company's five-year effort to shake up a rigid and poorly performing company. Starting with top management's public proclamation of "a time of self-criticism to discover what is wrong with us," the company has taken—and apparently stuck to—a number of tough decisions, including the following:

- Removing the date of hire from employee badges and abolishing the corresponding rule that no one could speak until those with more seniority had voiced their opinions first

- Rescinding the rule forbidding employees to drive competitors' cars

- Ordering everyone working on car design, from the top of the company to the bottom, to go "town watching"—visiting the tony sections of Tokyo to get ideas about the consumers who set the trends

- Borrowing ideas from rival Honda, including the styling of its corporate lobby showroom and the "idea contest" Honda uses to stimulate inventiveness among its engineers

- Allowing employees to dress casually (even in blue jeans) and work on flex-time schedules, and offering coed dorms to those workers who live in company-provided rooms

Already the changes are beginning to pay off, with dramatic new styling of cars that before were terminally boxy, and incipient though slow improvement in market share and profitability. And while the changes made so far have been difficult, Nissan management claims that the recovery will take even more of the same. Says president Yutaka Kume, "We are still only halfway through the turnaround of this company, and there are many more things to do. . . . [but] the momentum we have generated is unstoppable."

MANAGERS ARE MORE LIKELY
TO ACT ON THE FACTS WHEN THEY:

- Explicitly understand "the way we do business around here"

- Address whether "the company way" matches the requirements for market success

- Make a conscious decision about whether it is worthwhile for this organization to change the way it does business

- Honestly face who loses in a change (including themselves)

- Take the gut tests to see if they will be willing to act consistently to support the changes indicated by the facts

CHAPTER TWO

—————————— ✦ ✦ ✦ ——————————

We Know What the Facts Are

*The human mind treats a new idea the way the body
treats a new protein; it rejects it.*

—BIOLOGIST P. B. MEDAWAR

THE ASSUMPTION:

We know what the facts are.

THE REALITY:

People often don't see what is right in front of
them.

THE RESULT:

Signs of important new opportunities or threats
are missed until it's too late.

SOME COMMON SIGNS WHEN YOU AREN'T SEEING ALL THE FACTS

- All the data are exactly as you expect, all the time.

- The data always fit—although sometimes it takes a little time to redefine the question.

- Some of the data don't fit—but generally those are the "outliers" that therefore shouldn't be considered.

- You read or hear something that makes you feel vaguely uncomfortable.

- You read or hear something that makes you angry and defensive.

- You feel uncomfortable because the data are breaking in a way that will not meet the expectations or preferences of someone with more power than you.

- You sometimes feel like you've been blindsided by changes in the marketplace that your competitors have already used to their own advantage.

Few people are likely to forget the tragedy of the space shuttle Challenger, with its crew of seven, including a civilian public-school teacher. On January 28, 1986, as the nation watched the highly publicized launch, the booster rocket designed to carry the craft aloft blew apart, killing everyone on board.

How did it happen? The technical details are fairly clear. As the subsequent investigation showed, the O-rings and joint seals in the solid rocket booster could not withstand the abnormally cold temperatures on the launchpad, resulting in the explosion of the spacecraft.

More mysterious is how a group of dedicated professionals—engineers and managers at Morton Thiokol, maker of the booster rocket, and officials at NASA—allowed the launch recommendation to go forward. All were aware of data that suggested an increased risk of O-ring malfunction at temperatures below 53 degrees Fahrenheit: two Thiokol engineers used these data to argue passionately that the launch should be delayed. Yet over the course of the pre-launch meetings, the normal safety protocol became inverted; instead of having to prove that the mission *should* proceed, the criteria subtly shifted to requiring proof that the O-rings would *not* hold in cold weather. Such proof was impossible, and the mission was therefore approved.

The lessons of the Challenger launch are as important to corporate control as they are to mission control, for they illustrate how expectations and preferences can lead decision makers to ignore vital data and distort the facts. Whether the business at hand is launching rockets into space or space heaters into the marketplace, the result is the same: a greater risk of failure and lost opportunities.

OUT OF SIGHT, OUT OF MIND

The people who run organizations typically assume that they use the available facts when they make decisions. But no one

47

can operate on the basis of the facts that aren't seen. And facts frequently do go unseen due to the power of personal expectations and preferences to block out or distort information from the world around us. The net effect is the same as not having the data at all.

Expectations serve as unconscious filters, permitting entry to data that fit with a preexisting picture of the world while preventing passage of those data that don't, which is why many companies fail to see new competitors as serious threats until it is too late. Because the filtering of discordant facts isn't conscious, its effects on the decision-making process are particularly dangerous.

Preferences, in contrast, serve as conscious filters; the unwelcome data *are* recognized—and then are rejected. An example of preferences at work was the decision of a senior manager at GM who, having been shown a sales forecast of 3,000 cars for the first year of a new model, ordered it redone to show projected sales of 7,000—and thereby an acceptable return on investment. (The company subsequently sold 3,000.) When preferences take control, we dismiss or distort what we don't like, often with a display of anger. Though preferences are easier to ferret out than expectations, they're even more pesky because of our strong investment in maintaining them.

Keeping the cognitive filters of expectations and preferences from getting in the way begins with an appreciation of how the mind screens and distorts the facts. Listening to what you don't want to hear is *not* a natural skill; it takes conscious effort to consider data that otherwise would be screened out or interpreted incorrectly. Such an effort is inherently unsettling, but the alternative is worse: the risk that decisions are made on the basis of only those facts that resonate with our minds and emotions.

GREAT EXPECTATIONS

Psychologists have long known that people tend to be most able to see and hear what they *expect* to see and hear. The corollary is that they tend not to perceive what is unexpected—when people expect to see one thing, they will rarely see what they do not expect, even when it is right before their eyes. In short, in the presence of the unexpected, people typically do one of two things: They either entirely block out the data that don't fit, or they unconsciously massage the data to match their expectations. Or as Winston Churchill once said, "People sometimes stumble over the truth, but usually they pick themselves up and hurry about their business."

Anatomy of an Expectation

An expectation is part of a mental model that describes how things do or should work. It might concern a simple action, such as predicting how people typically behave in a given situation. Or it might involve a complex set of assumptions, about the mechanics of the global economy, for example, and the flow of goods, capital, and information within it. When the task is to predict how a company will achieve success, the models that businesspeople carry in their heads typically include expectations about what customers want or could want, what competitors are likely to do, and what it will take for everyone else in the organization to help serve the customers and beat the competition.

These models provide an orientation and serve as an economical way of making sense of a complex world. Without them, people would be overwhelmed by more data than they could possibly process. Just think about what it's like to be transferred to an entirely new business or to take a course in an entirely new field. In the early stages, you are likely to be disoriented and maybe even anxious. Eventually, to your great relief, you "get it": you learn, you discover, and the pieces come together. Those pieces comprise your mental model, and your subsequent awareness of "what goes where" allows you

49

to tend to the business at hand economically. For better or worse, your expectations are set.

Once in place, however, your expectations are in control. To appreciate the power of this control, visualize a deck of playing cards. If someone flashed individual cards from this deck quickly on a screen before you, you would anticipate the hearts and diamonds to be red and the spades and clubs to be black. So what would happen if someone slipped a red six of spades into the deck? When psychologists actually did this in a now-classic experiment, most people "saw" either a red six of hearts or a black six of spades. Their expectations outweighed the facts.

Misreading a playing card is not a big deal. But when the data being ignored or distorted to fit expectations are crucial to business decisions, the cognitive filtering process becomes much more important. Consider the almost twenty-year head start the Big Three U.S. automakers handed to German and Japanese manufacturers in the compact-car market when they largely ignored the threat posed by these foreign entrants.

See No Evil, Hear No Evil

When Volkswagen introduced the Beetle to the U.S. market in 1950, the company sold only 300 cars. U.S. carmakers (and many consumers) joked that the "bug" was little more than a toy. Few worried that the toy would become a threat to the industry because, as a 1952 Ford report explained, "to the average American, our present car and its size represent an outward symbol of prestige and well-being." Eight years later, however, more than 100,000 Beetles were rolling onto American roadways annually, and by 1966 that number had quadrupled. But despite the ever-increasing number of Beetles on U.S. soil, a favorite joke in Detroit concerned the three most

overrated things in America: Southern cooking, home sex, and
. . . foreign cars.

Detroit similarly ignored another group of cars that began
arriving eight years after the Beetle: the first wave of the new
Japanese imports. Detroit's initial disdain of its new competitors may have been somewhat understandable, for although
the Beetle was merely funny-looking, the Japanese cars were
totally unsuited to American roads.

Take the first Toyotas. Introduced to U.S. consumers in
1958, these cars were so miserably designed and built that the
company pulled them off the market and didn't reintroduce
them until 1964. The early Datsuns, produced by Nissan and
introduced at about the same time as the first Toyotas, also
fared poorly in the U.S and for good reason: they arrived with
underpowered engines, undersized batteries, weak brakes, and
an involuntary climate-control system—the engine—that made
the cars so hot year-round that Datsun salesmen nicknamed
them the "mobile coffins." Faced with clearly deficient cars,
some Nissan employees stationed in the U.S. speculated that
the corporate executives in Tokyo had selected the name "Datsun" for the U.S.-destined cars to protect the Nissan name in
the likely case of failure. (The name was finally changed to
Nissan about twenty years later.)

But despite their inauspicious beginnings, the Japanese
manufacturers were able to adjust their cars faster than the
American manufacturers could adjust their perceptions. The
rest of the story is well known. By 1979, imports accounted
for over 20 percent of the U.S. market. Yet even then, many
in Detroit continued to interpret the increasing import penetration as partly a matter of luck that could not have been
predicted. Lee Iacocca, for example, suggests that the foreign
car companies didn't have better insight into U.S. consumers,
they just happened to have had the right cars when the Shah
of Iran was overthrown in 1979 and oil supplies became threat-
ened. But whether or when the Shah would fall was only one

aspect of a long-term trend that favored higher-quality small cars. After all, the instabilities in the Middle East had been painfully apparent since the oil embargo of 1973. And fuel efficiency aside, increasing numbers of consumers had begun to see imports as a better value in general: more car for the money in terms of comfort, reliability, and quality.

Similarly, as late as the mid-1980s, GM interpreted its consumer research as showing that the people who bought imports were snobs. Out of all the interviews they conducted in California, the one remembered—and retold—the most was the young woman who reportedly said: "If I had a blind date and he showed up in a Honda, I'd know we were going to a nice restaurant and then doing something fun afterwards. If he showed up in a Chevy, I'd figure that we were going to Jack in the Box." Their conclusion? That no Chevrolet could draw these customers back to GM and that the company would therefore need to invest in a new brand, one with more snob appeal. (The new brand became Saturn.) Once again, the data that were getting through the screen were being forced to fit, like the red six of spades. The reason that Chevy's past import fighters—the Vega, Chevette, and Cavalier—had failed was not because they were called "Chevrolet." It was because they were, in the words of Maryann Keller, an industry analyst who follows GM, "poor imitations" of their imported competition.

Today, of course, no one in Detroit is likely to ignore colleagues on other continents or distort the available data quite so dramatically; the expectations of U.S. automakers have been rudely adjusted. But in the 1950s and 1960s (and possibly straight through the 1970s) the belief held by the Big Three that only Detroit could give Americans the kind of cars they wanted provided important air cover to the new entrants. Or as Yutaka Katayama (the Nissan man who pried the Fair Lady nameplates off the first 240 Zs) counseled his American associates during the 1960s: "What we should do is get better and creep up slowly, so we'll be good—and the customer will think we're good—before Detroit even knows about us."

The U.S. automakers aren't the only companies that have been trapped by their own expectations. It happens in all industries and in all cultures. In fact, while Katayama was taking advantage of the opportunities created by the expectations of his American competitors, he was fighting the expectations held within his own company. His descriptions of the requirements for competing in the U.S. market seemed so outlandish—even improper—that the initial response from headquarters to virtually any Katayama initiative was to dismiss his data—and reject his recommendations.

Nevertheless, Katayama persisted and continually barraged Tokyo with information that the executives at headquarters considered too strange to be believed. Take Katayama's recommendation for more powerful engines. With their displacement of just 1,000 cc, Nissan's export engines were even smaller than those used in the Beetle (1,300 cc) and were almost laughable in comparison with the engines used in small U.S. cars (5,000 to 6,000 cc). But the Japanese road system at the time was so poor that it was difficult for the Nissan managers sitting in Tokyo to imagine that acceleration and engine power could really be that important to cracking the U.S. market.

Then there was the very odd American desire to have cars with carpet mats attached to the floor. The Japanese, typically fastidious about cleaning their cars, wanted removable carpet pads that could be readily shampooed and vacuumed; Americans wanted the convenience of mats that stayed put. Most peculiar of all, though, was the notion that Americans wanted trucks equipped with the amenities of passenger cars—softer suspensions, better upholstery, even air conditioning. In Japan, trucks were for hauling things, cars for transporting people. Why would anyone mix the two? Not only was it unheard of, it was downright unseemly.

It took him almost a decade, but Katayama won the race: he convinced his colleagues about the nature of the U.S. market *before* his American competitors fully appreciated the threat Nissan and other firms like it represented. That U.S. manufacturers now are acutely sensitive to foreign competition merely shows that over time (and under assault) expectations do change. Anticipating such change *prior* to the assault is therefore the challenge. The question is always this: What are the blind spots created by today's expectations, and will we see around these blind spots before being done in by them?

The Enemy Within

In all the above cases, expectations of certain data caused smart managers to ignore facts that didn't conform to their preexisting world view. Their expectations blocked out selected information about competitors, customers, and employees, masking reality until it came crashing through the door. This blocking process is most likely—and therefore most dangerous—when a threat advances slowly, because the accumulating damage is then harder to detect. That's what happened to the U.S. automakers as they consistently underestimated their new Japanese and German competitors over a twenty-year period. By contrast, companies like Nissan faced a sharper reality: The Japanese market was limited, and they needed to learn quickly how to win in the U.S. market while the giant remained asleep.

What some call the "boiled frog effect" is one way to explain the difference between the U.S. and Japanese situations. If you drop a frog into a beaker and slowly heat the bottom with a Bunsen burner, the frog will perish. But if you first heat the water to a roaring boil and then add the frog, the animal will leap out, perhaps a bit worse for wear, but alive and wiser to the ways of the world. Expectations typically thrive without challenge in slow-boil situations, increasing the chances that warning signs go unnoticed until it's too late.

Bringing Expectations to the Surface

Expectations are an essential part of managing, of course; if managers didn't have a point of view, no decisions would ever get made. The challenge therefore is to figure out if there isn't a different way of looking at the world that would invalidate the assumptions that guide today's decisions. Consider what would have happened if:

- Macy's managers, during the early 1980s, had challenged their long-standing premise that profits come from controlling costs (minimizing inventories, preventing inventory shrink, and legislating efficiency). They might have thought about shopping from the customer's point of view before Nordstrom's, with its obsession with service, gobbled up market share on the West Coast.

- Xerox executives, during the 1970s, had challenged their assumption that no one wanted slow but cheap and reliable copiers that could make between 8 and 20 copies per minute when large Xerox machines could make up to 120 copies per minute. Chances are, they never would have given away the lucrative small-copier end of the market to Savin, a domestic upstart, and its Japanese partner Ricoh. In fact, long after the Savin 750 was introduced in 1975, Xerox still did not consistently include its growing Japanese competition in its internal reports of market share. And the company consistently rejected plans from its partner, Fuji-Xerox, and from its outside advisors to go after this new market aggressively with a better small copier.

- The major integrated steel mills, beginning in the late 1960s, had questioned the "given" that their customers would continue to pay top dollar for rod, bar, and wire products even though lower-cost—albeit lower-grade—equivalents were becoming widely available from the new minimills dotting the U.S. landscape. If they had, they probably wouldn't have invested as heavily in basic steel-making capacity such as iron ore mines, iron pelletizing facilities, blast furnaces, and basic oxygen furnaces. The money saved could have been used instead to upgrade the finishing mills for the more complex products that the minimills couldn't make and that represented an important part of the industry's defense against imports.

Turning your assumptions inside out is not only a good defense against being blindsided by competitors or left behind in the wake of a changing customer base. It also opens a path that can lead to innovative products and services and a head start on competitors. Consider some classic examples:

- The traditional way airlines fill planes is to take reservations, sell tickets in advance, and assign seats. But what if you questioned whether this was the only way to run an airline? What if you ran an airline almost like a city bus? Answer: You would have developed a new type of air travel—the once highly lucrative Eastern Shuttle (later, the Trump Shuttle).

- The traditional style of selling women's stockings was one per leg, sold in department stores. What if you broke all the rules and made a product that hardly ever runs, then reduced the price drastically, packaged the product in a silly plastic "eggshell," and sold it in supermarkets? You would have L'eggs, a runaway success that was brought to the market not by a new player, but by Hanes, which still sells its other brands in department stores.

- The unwritten first rule of thumb in commercial real estate development was don't build if you don't already have a tenant. Turn those ideas upside down, as real estate developer Trammell Crow did, and you would have made a fortune building warehouses on speculation and selling them to Texas companies that needed more storage space but were reluctant to sign leases before the buildings were constructed.

In short, making expectations explicit so that they can be examined is a prerequisite for being able to see and use a greater portion of the available facts. You can't buck human nature and purge your mind of all its models of the world, nor would you ever want to. But you can infinitely raise your level of awareness by constantly asking yourself what you might not be seeing or hearing, and by being attentive to the feelings of surprise or discomfort that signal an expectation under attack. And you can actively create situations in which inside views are challenged (for example, by requesting someone— but not always the same person—to take the role of "devil's advocate") and in which outside views are solicited (for example, by inviting people with different perspectives to share their ideas).

PRIDE AND PREFERENCES

Whereas expectations prevent us from seeing what we don't want to see and hearing what we don't want to hear, personal preferences are a more active way of selectively blocking offensive data or reshaping them according to our emotional terrain. And although much of management theory is based on the notion of unbiased, detached consideration of the facts, few corporate veterans would argue that such preferences—and the pride and other emotions they engender—are ever checked outside the workplace door.

Anatomy of a Preference

In some ways, a preference is an expectation fueled by ego because it represents a desire to hear a certain answer and a corresponding unwillingness to hear anything else. Because of the explicit desire to hear only certain things, preferences, unlike expectations, do not work imperceptibly to block the offending data. Instead, information that violates a preference is usually accompanied by strong emotion—and often by an equally strong desire to put things back the way they were before the new data were introduced. That was the situation at a company in a highly cyclical business, oil-field equipment, which, during one of the industry upturns in the early 1980s, forbade the use of the word "cyclical" in any discussions or documents about its strategy or potential investments. (The rule held but the company didn't when the market predictably turned down again.)

Not all preferences are bad, of course. Some are essential to running an organization because they provide the backbone both to the values that the firm uses to differentiate itself and its products and to the decision rules that the firm's members use to conduct their business lives. In extreme forms, however, these same preferences make it impossible for individuals and groups to deal with unwelcome information. For those great leaders whose instincts and vision far outreach those of the people around them, this is not a major problem. For the rest of us, however, the power of preferences to block out or distort information can lead to irrational or counterproductive decisions.

The Power of Preference

Constancy of vision is a double-edged sword: it can propel a company to new heights or send it to the depths of disaster. Consider Edwin Land, the founder of the Polaroid Corporation. From the time he started out in a dark basement apartment in New York, which he used as both his living quarters and his chemistry laboratory, through his founding and chairmanship of Polaroid, Land was guided by one preference: elegance of technology.

But the same preference that gave the world instant photography was also responsible for costly corporate blunders, for Land's response to information that went against his preferences reputedly ranged from frosty silence to visible anger. Take the focusing mechanism for Polaroid's breakthrough camera, the SX-70, introduced in 1972. Land's focusing system was the essence of technical elegance—the photographer simply turned the lens until the image seen through the viewfinder went from fuzzy to suddenly sharp. For people like Land with good vision, the device was perfect. But for those who were nearsighted or who wore bifocals or thick lenses, the shift from fuzzy to sharp could be very difficult to detect.

Those critical of the focusing mechanism, however, had to brave Land's wrath. To the optical engineers who developed an alternative design, Land retorted that the consumers must be taught to use the viewfinder he had designed and that the marketing department was responsible for making this happen. When a half year later John Wolbarst, head of customer service at Polaroid and former editor of *Modern Photography,* used reports and transcripts from customer interviews to argue for the new focusing system, Land held to his original view. Even though the alternative viewfinder was finally accepted after still another six months, Land reportedly never spoke to Wolbarst again.

Land's confidence in himself and his preferences meant that he seldom sought contrary opinions on matters related to product design. (In fact, Land shunned market research. And while the hit rate of his instincts was uncommonly high, the practice hurt Polaroid in the development of Polavision, an instant moving-picture system that, though a technical marvel, could not compete with the then-emerging home videotape machines.)

Unlike Land, however, many managers with strong preferences do ask for other people's views. Often, however, they do not recognize that what they are really seeking is not new information but validation of their own preferences. Consider the case of Keith Dunn, a veteran executive of several large restaurant chains who broke from the pack to start his company, McGuffey's, a group of family restaurants headquartered in North Carolina. Dissatisfied with what he saw as the cycle of oppressive management and workers who simply go through the motions, Dunn set out to prove that the work environment in a restaurant could be fun. After three years of hard work and several McGuffey's restaurants up and going, Dunn distributed a one-page survey to the entire staff, asking for their views on working at McGuffey's. But Dunn's hopes for validation and support quickly evaporated as he reviewed the results:

> "With one of his partners by his side, he ripped open the first envelope as eagerly as a Broadway producer checking the reviews on opening night. His eyes zoomed directly to the question where employees were asked to rate the three owners' performance on a scale of one to ten. . . .

> "A zero. . . . 'Find out whose handwriting this is,' he told his partner, Richard Laibson.

> "He ripped another; zero again. And another. A two. 'We'll fire these people,' Dunn said. . . .

> "Soon he had vowed to fire 10% of his 230 employees."

As with Land, the message did get through the screen of expectations—Dunn clearly saw, but at first wasn't willing to accept, the data in front of him. And like Land, Dunn's angry response was a sure sign that his preferences were the next line of defense.

Facing Preferences: Let Your Emotions Be Your Guide

While challenges to expectations bring vague feelings of disorientation or discomfort, violations of preferences often lead to anger and frustration. Consider the case of a small, growing company in high-tech services that operated under the price umbrella of a major competitor. The smaller company believed that this competitor was going to increase prices by five percent plus inflation for the following year and then hold the prices even with inflation. After studying the market situation, however, a consultant to the smaller company became convinced that the competitor was actually likely to *drop* its prices at least five percent in real terms and then continue *lowering* prices at a less aggressive rate for the next five years.

Such a price drop had enormous implications. The smaller company would have to lower its prices too, which in turn would mean lowering costs. And lowering costs would require a massive restructuring and a complicated explanation to investors, both highly unpleasant tasks. So perhaps what transpired next was not surprising. Upon hearing the pricing predictions, the senior vice president of the smaller company turned beet red, withdrew a felt-tip pen from the breast pocket of his jacket, drew a large X over the pricing data page, ripped the page out of the presentation book, rolled it into a ball, and angrily declared the matter closed.

While the matter indeed remained closed within the smaller company, the large competitor went ahead and did the "inconceivable", dropping its prices not by five percent but by ten, and continuing with further cuts during the next five years. The result? The large competitor now has one less small competitor.

In this instance, the manager's anger should have been a tip-off that something was amiss; anything that triggers such a violent emotional response is suspect. In such situations, it's important to catch yourself and ask what would happen if the data making you so angry *were* correct. It's also important to create multiple opportunities to hear what you don't want to hear.

That's ultimately what Keith Dunn did after he realized that he was trying to run McGuffey's as an employee-oriented company without ever really talking to his employees. Now Dunn knows why exhortations to listen are next to useless without an understanding of one's own defenses against absorbing information that violates personal expectations and preferences. Or as Dunn puts it, "Listening is hard. . . . I have to hear the same thing five different times before my ego allows it to sink in. I don't give up easily. But if you hear something in enough places, you get the message."

Meeting Other People's Preferences

Sometimes other people's expectations and preferences can significantly influence one's own cognitive filters; the more severe the pressure, the greater the likelihood of filtering or distortion. The ill-fated launch of the space shuttle Challenger illustrates just how powerful such pressure from outside sources can be. Or as the Rogers Commission, which investigated the incident, concluded in its formal report, "Thiokol management reversed its position and recommended the launch of 51-L . . . in order to accommodate a major customer."

A deeper look into the pre-launch decision process for Challenger shows the root of the problem. When the Thiokol team made its initial recommendation not to launch, representatives of NASA made their displeasure clear: one remarked that he was "appalled," and another expressed his dismay over a launch that might be delayed until April, three months away. That started a chain reaction, culminating in a discussion in which the Thiokol team of managers and engineers withdrew to discuss the problem without the participation of NASA personnel. As the Thiokol group leaned toward reversing its no-go recommendation, two of the engineers tried desperately to have the original recommendation upheld. In testimony to the Rogers Commission, Roger Boisjoly, one of the engineers, described what happened next:

"Those of us who opposed the launch continued to speak out. . . . And we were attempting to go back and rereview and try to make clear what we were trying to get across, and we couldn't understand why it was going to be reversed. So we spoke out and tried to explain once again the effects of low temperature. Arnie [Arnold Thompson, one of the other Thiokol engineers] actually got up from his position which was down the table and walked up the table and put a quarter pad down in front of the table, in front of the management folks, and tried to sketch out once again what his concern was with the [nozzle] joint, and when he realized he wasn't getting through, he just stopped.

"I tried one more time with the photos. I grabbed the photos and I went up and discussed the photos once again and tried to make the point that it was my opinion from actual observations that temperature was indeed a discriminator and we should not ignore the physical evidence we had observed. . . . I also stopped when it was apparent that I couldn't get anybody to listen. . . .

"I really did all that I could to stop the launch. . . ."

The process was very subtle, and it was only afterward that one of the pivotal participants, Jerry Lund, Thiokol's manager of engineering, realized that the usual standards for a launch had shifted—the burden of proof had shifted from justifying a launch to justifying a delay. The combination of expectations and preferences, though subtle, proved deadly.

• • •

An executive director of a trade association heard a speech by two psychologists about the uses of upward feedback. Inspired, he went back to his office, designed a confidential form, and circulated it to his staff. Under the protection of anonymity, his employees no longer felt that they had to obey the signals, and they told him what they really thought—which was not what he wanted to hear. Convinced by his expectations and preferences that somehow the evaluations he had received were neither fair nor credible, he reprinted the forms and sent them out again, but with the following note attached:

"I'd like you to fill out these forms again—and this time rate me accurately!"

The power of expectations and preferences is difficult to overestimate.

THE FACTS ARE MORE LIKELY TO BE SEEN WHEN MANAGERS:

- Make their own expectations and preferences explicit to themselves

- Try to be clear about the expectations and preferences of those who have more power than they, so they don't inadvertently censor the data to meet these expectations and preferences

- Use their feelings of discomfort or anger as signals of the presence of unexpected or undesired data

- Occasionally assign a "devil's advocate" (but not always the same person) to challenge the current or emerging consensus

- Solicit views from people who are likely to bring fresh or unusual perspectives

- Find ways to play "what if" with unpleasant data

- Keep track of "outliers" or "wrong" data to see if more evidence like them appears, and if the implications are important enough, *actively* seek other data like them

CHAPTER THREE

———————◆ ◆ ◆———————

We Have All the Facts
We Need

*I don't want any yes men around me. I want people
who will tell me the truth even if it costs them their jobs.*

—SAM GOLDWYN

THE ASSUMPTION:

We have all the facts we need.

THE REALITY:

Many of the people who have the facts don't
speak up.

THE RESULT:

The managers are the last to know about some
developing problem or threat, or never know
about some potential opportunity.

SOME COMMON SIGNS OF A
BLOCKED INFORMATION FLOW

- You don't have a constant stream of ideas from customers, suppliers, or employees (although competitors seem to).

- Few people inside the organization seem to have any concerns or ideas about alternative approaches, or at least they never express any.

- People joke about "CLMs"—career limiting moves—when they are asked to express their opinions.

- Techniques like management by walking around or suggestion boxes rarely provide new information or ideas.

- Despite invitations to speak up, you have the vague sense that people are censoring what they tell you.

- Most of what people tell you confirms what you think.

- Rocking the boat is seen and responded to as a sign of someone who is disloyal or a poor team player.

- Almost all decisions are made with a minimum of dispute or debate.

- Somehow, outspoken people never seem to get very far in the organization or have to be absolutely outstanding to do so.

- You find sometimes that you're the last to know about something important.

In the secluded pine forests of Maine, the members of the New England offices of a large accounting firm meet each summer for a three-day retreat. Who wouldn't enjoy this respite from the office, complete with lovely scenery, fresh air, and contemplative atmosphere? The only problem is that the firm holds its retreats on weekends, a fact that some of the more junior accountants with young families and heavy travel schedules find burdensome.

Although everyone knows that the managing partner, Hal O'Keefe, regards these retreats as highly important, one year rumors of discontent finally bubbled up to the executive suite. To determine the facts, O'Keefe asked, at the tail end of a management meeting, whether it really was true that some people were dissatisfied with the retreat schedule. While the senior managers in the meeting had no more information than O'Keefe, most of the middle managers present knew the answer to his question. Even so, they either remained silent or assured him that the last retreat had been a stunning success. O'Keefe listened carefully but neither pressed the question nor explained why he was asking. The result: O'Keefe did not get the facts he was seeking and no change in the schedule was considered.

What went wrong? O'Keefe had been a straight shooter and had made an honest and clear request for new information. But in fact, honest requests often don't beget honest answers, for there are usually real and perceived costs that inhibit people from offering their ideas and perspectives. For this reason, simply inviting challenge and soliciting comments sometimes isn't enough. And when it isn't, potentially vital information remains withheld by the people on whom the organization depends—employees, customers, distributors, and suppliers.

The root of the problem lies in what might be called the "First Law of Information Flow," which states that the likely rewards to the information provider must exceed their likely

71

costs. In other words, people won't speak up unless there's something in it for them. The bad news is that in most organizations, the potential costs are high, and the rewards, if they exist at all, are trivial. The good news is that it's more than possible to change the equation in favor of those who have important information to offer.

BEYOND THE 50–50 PROPOSITION

Many managers believe that if they do their part—invite people into their offices, wander around and talk to everyone, conduct surveys, install suggestion boxes—those who have something to say will speak up. "Hey, my door is open any time," these managers say. "Drop by and tell me what's on your mind." But such seemingly straightforward gestures are often insufficient or even counterproductive, for few people will speak their minds when the odds of a positive return are slim.

Take the administrative assistant who works for a sales manager who invites comments but is known to act on other people's ideas only rarely and, in the few instances when he does, almost always takes full credit for himself. The administrative assistant has noticed that marginal accounts are receiving the same energy as the mother lodes, and that the reps are scurrying inefficiently from one end of the region to the other as they try to give each account equal treatment. If the call requirements were changed and the compensation structure reorganized, she speculates, everyone would be much more productive and could add significantly to the company's profits.

Great idea. But what's the probability that she will share it with her boss? Go back to the First Law of Information Flow. The administrative assistant not only has low odds of a positive outcome but also runs the risk of wasting her own time and possibly incurring the greater cost of being labeled a troublemaker. She'll therefore probably decide to bite her tongue and continue to earn her paychecks without rocking the boat.

From the outside, the logic behind the administrative assistant's decision to remain silent is sound. From the sales manager's perspective, however, the decision to withhold information that could improve business performance might seem unprofessional or worse. After all, the sales manager might figure, he did *his* 50 percent by opening the door; the rest of the burden for completing the communication should lie with his subordinate.

As this hypothetical situation illustrates, though, "shoulds" don't count when there isn't an attractive outcome for the person with the information. Nor are neutral outcomes good enough, because most people will remain silent even when the costs and rewards of speaking up are a wash. The onus therefore falls on those who need the information to create the expectation of a net positive outcome for sharing news and ideas, even when the news is bad or the ideas are disruptive to the status quo.

When the information holders don't perceive any advantage in making a contribution, the hidden costs to the company are often significant. Employees, customers, distributors, and suppliers fight the daily front-line battles and know their parts of the business better than anyone else. Top management can theorize and speculate from sunrise to sundown about the way things are supposed to be, but in fact only those closest to the action see the details of what's working and what isn't, what might be at risk of attack and what might be the basis for increased profitability. Take, for example, a few of the ways that the front-line information resulting from customer calls to 800 lines has led to product improvements: Pillsbury changed the consistency of its Best Sugar Cookie dough so it can be rolled out and cut with cookie cutters as well as dropped from a spoon; General Electric modified the buzzer on its

73

clothes dryers so it can be turned off; and Warner-Lambert is considering a new product based on customer comments that Efferdent, its denture cleanser, is just terrific at removing toilet bowl stains.

Tapping such extended networks of "ten thousand eyes and ears" therefore gives companies the benefits of a grassroots intelligence system. In most organizations, however, taking advantage of this intelligence requires reworking the communication equation by taking one or more of the following actions:

- Reducing the penny-ante costs

- Decreasing the risk of catastrophic losses

- Increasing the rewards

For some companies, making these kinds of changes can be wrenching, because they require a radical break from the old "50–50" proposition. But the pain is well worth it, for such changes allow managers to stay current with information from the front lines, instead of being "the last to know."

REDUCING THE PENNY-ANTE COSTS

Minor costs in the communication equation include the time and expense it takes to pass along information. For an employee, such costs may be the requirement of booking an appointment, developing a presentation, or preparing a memo for a senior official. For a customer, they may be the expense of an envelope and stamp or of a toll call, or the time to fill out a form or write a letter. And for suppliers and distributors, minor costs might involve attending additional meetings or tracking down the right person to discuss problems or new ideas.

When Trivial Costs Break the Bank

Minor costs are easy to dismiss from the point of view of the information seeker—after all, they really *are* trivial. More to the point, most managers hope that those who have important information care enough about the organization to incur a small out-of-pocket expense. Nonetheless, seemingly trivial costs can make the difference between information volunteered and information withheld, especially when it's easier for the information holder to switch rather than fight; that is, to withdraw rather than speak up. People who have many other good options that are easily exercised—purchasers of breakfast cereals, temporary office workers in an overheated local economy, suppliers and distributors with too much demand and not enough capacity—have relatively low switching costs. So do other employees who, rather than speaking up, can "switch off"—do the minimum in their jobs and no more. For all these groups, any but the most trivial expense will be *the* obstacle to speaking up, because it simply will be easier for them to go elsewhere or to keep their ideas to themselves.

Sound farfetched? Think about the last time you were angered by the service in a restaurant or had an idea for improving a product you regarded as fatally flawed in its current form. Chances are, unless you were patronizing the only restaurant of its type in town, you didn't complain to the manager—you simply began eating at the establishment across the street. And unless the stores in your town stock only one brand per category, you probably neither called nor wrote the manufacturer to share your insights or experiences; you just tried a new brand. In short, you likely did not share your ideas, but you probably shifted your business.

Studies of consumer complaints show the same pattern. One suggests that only 2 percent of dissatisfied customers complain—while 34 percent switch brands and 4 percent stop buying that kind of product altogether; another indicates that 4 percent complain—and somewhere between 60 and 90 percent go elsewhere. Though the exact numbers differ, the bottom line is the same: just because no one is complaining doesn't mean that everyone is happy and lacks ideas for improvement.

The situation is not that different for employees, who may have good ideas but find the presentation requirements sufficiently burdensome that they decide not to speak up. That was one of the conclusions physics professor Richard Feynman reached during an investigation into why the solid rocket boosters in NASA space shuttles became a little out of round after each use. Having been told by the manager of the area that the problem was due to mistakes by the workers in the solid rocket booster assembly area, Feynman went to talk with the workers themselves, after which he came to a markedly different conclusion:

> "Mr. Lamberth [the manager of the area] didn't really know what happened . . . [because] he never talked to them [the workmen] directly. . . . They had noticed all kinds of problems and had all kinds of ideas on how to fix them, but no one had paid much attention to them. *The reason was: Any observations had to be reported in writing, and a lot of these guys didn't know how to write good memos."*

In fact, as Feynman discovered, the mistakes were due not to lazy people but to incorrect instructions in the procedures manual itself. The workers in the booster area saw the problems and had figured out possible solutions but simply found it too costly, in terms of time and energy, to try to communicate their ideas to others.

Nor is the situation much different for suppliers and distributors who aren't dependent on your company. If they can do well despite your inefficiencies or have a waiting list for their services, they may either continue to do business with you without contributing their suggestions or begin to shift their services to others in need of their wares.

In all these cases, the problem is the same: what looks like small costs to the information seeker may be just enough to keep the information holder from speaking up. If it's easier to switch out or switch off, the information and ideas are unlikely to be communicated.

Making It Easy to Volunteer Information

Fortunately, trivial costs are not very difficult to remove; mostly it's a matter of shifting small burdens from those who have the information to those who want it. Whether you're dealing with employees, customers, distributors, or suppliers, the way to reduce these penny-ante costs is therefore pretty basic: imagine all the little obstacles that could prevent someone from speaking up, and find ways to remove them. (But remember that reducing the trivial costs will only make a difference if the risk of catastrophic losses is low and the odds of a positive outcome are reasonable.)

DECREASING THE RISK OF
CATASTROPHIC LOSSES

In theory, information holders who cannot easily exit the situation and whose futures are therefore inextricably linked with those of the information seekers have a stake in speaking up and should be first in line to share what they know. But often these same people face a significant barrier to contributing their information: the fear of retribution, or what is commonly thought of as the shoot-the-messenger syndrome. Faced with the possibility of losing some of the benefits of the time and effort they have invested in their jobs or businesses, people in this situation will now switch off rather than fight, and the flow of real news reduces to a trickle.

Concerns about possible retribution may be felt by anyone dependent on a company, including, in some circumstances, its suppliers, distributors, and customers. But the information holders most typically inhibited by such concerns are the organization's employees. Even where employees truly do have other employment options, the *perceived* switching costs of finding and starting a new job can make them react *as though* they have no other real alternatives. Corporate rhetoric about "open environments" or "family feelings" aside, savvy employees are usually very wary about the potential price of speaking up.

How savvy employees learn to play the information game varies from company to company and country to country. At a major Japanese company, for example, Gary Katzenstein, an American participating in an employee-exchange program, was shocked to find that his colleagues were openly critical of the company, but only after working hours when they had imbibed enough alcohol to be (or claim to be) drunk. By the next morning, however, all memory of such comments would be disavowed. After all, the concerns had been uttered when everyone was drunk, and of course no one could remember anything that had been said.

Even when the request for information is sincere and would be acted on, as was the case with Hal O'Keefe in the opening example of this chapter, the perceived risk has the same effect: given the choice between rocking the boat and taking the corporate equivalent of the fifth amendment, most people will take the fifth.

When Silence Is Golden

In some organizations, the costs of volunteering information becomes the stuff of legend. Take the story told about Joseph

Butare, one of the presidents with the Conifer Group, a chain of Massachusetts banks specializing in community banking. When the Bank of New England acquired Conifer in 1986, Butare and the other Conifer presidents reportedly were promised continued autonomy in the way they ran their local operations. Concerned about how this agreement was working, Butare made an appointment to see Walter Connolly, president of the parent company. As a former senior executive tells the story, "Joe said he was going to have a talk with Walter. . . . He wasn't happy with the way things were going and he felt he could be utilized better. We laughed. You don't go to Walter with things like that." According to the executive, Butare was fired the same day.

In most organizations, though, bad news is not rebuffed quite so violently, but often just as effectively. Here are a few ways this is done:

- "You're wasting my time—you don't know what you're talking about! I thought you had a better understanding of this industry than that!"

- "I'm very surprised to hear you say these things! This is a time when we all have to pull together to get the job done!"

- "Hey, whose side are you on, anyway? We like team players around here, you know."

- "I'm tired of hearing your excuses. Now get back to work."

- "Why are you always so negative?"

Statements like these, and the displays of anger or irritation that typically accompany them, are very powerful. They tell the information giver that he or she may have already committed a "CLM"—career-limiting move. And they each imply a serious criticism: either the information is badly flawed, indicating that the giver is none too bright; or that the giver, though competent, has questionable loyalties or abilities as a team player. These are the real catastrophic losses that people fear: the risk of burning up goodwill and its associated advantages, such as promotions, assignments, compensation, or various other goodies that the listener controls.

Disloyalty Tests and Teamwork Traps

Conceptually, both loyalty and teamwork require vigorous debate, even confrontation. Dissent, after all, is often the ultimate act of allegiance. Yet many managers routinely conduct loyalty tests that send clear messages to potential contrarians or use the goal of frictionless teamwork to regulate who can speak up and what they can say. The dilemma is all the more difficult because many people are not very skilled at expressing their concerns gracefully or constructively, and therefore come across as disruptive or hostile even when their intentions are good and their news is important.

In some organizations, the methods of enforcing "good" team behavior can be quite extreme. At a military nuclear production plant near Fernald, Ohio, for example, psychiatric care was ordered for a worker who complained about emergency preparations based on his observation of an accidental release of uranium into the atmosphere and the response that followed. The pattern extended beyond this one worker; workers with safety complaints at three other similar plants run for the government by private contractors were also directed to seek psychological help. But the nuclear weapons industry is not unique. Sending employees to a whole range of counseling services and "charm schools" can be used to discourage a wide variety of maverick-like behaviors, despite the fact that understanding the information and ideas being shared may clearly be in the organization's best interests.

At one electronics company, for example, an engineer who sought to identify and solve inefficient practices, such as cannibalizing products almost ready for shipping so that their parts could be used for other orders, was also rewarded by an all-expenses-paid trip to a psychiatrist's office. But the effects of the trip had more to do with what he learned about organizational politics than about his own psychological dynamics: "I had really cared about the place and had taken the lead role on a number of highly successful projects," he explains. "But after they sent me to the psychiatrist, I completely changed my behavior. I disengaged, just switched off my initiative. So when I got a direct order, I did it, but otherwise I did the very minimum. When I saw problems develop, as I often did, I no longer tried to fix them. And do you know what happened? They loved me again! They liked me better when I was doing nothing than when I was adding profit dollars to the company! So I became like everyone else there—I did the minimum and I did just fine."

In most cases, however, the message is both less extreme and more subtle. Look at what happened to Cassandra Diaz, director of marketing for a customized software business, a division of a large publishing company. Known for her energetic, sometimes iconoclastic style, Diaz saw her appointment to the division's executive committee as a chance to help bring an out-of-control operation back to planet Earth. The need, as she saw it, was urgent, for the division was about to exceed even its previous record annual loss. And it was no wonder: Product line managers were spending all their budgeted funds, even though they were unlikely to achieve even half of their projected revenues. The sales force was in complete disarray because the reps had no idea of what they should be selling or who constituted their primary customers. New projects were being proposed and approved without any clear link to the current strategy. Pricing was chaotic. In short, Diaz concluded, the division would continue to lose massive amounts of money until management made radical and wrenching changes.

Diaz, having set out to staunch the division's flow of red ink, pushed the division's general manager and fellow executive committee members to face the issues. But despite her efforts, nothing happened. Finally, it seemed that all her hard work was about to pay off—her boss summoned the entire executive committee to what he billed as a "mission-critical meeting."

To Diaz's amazement, however, the purpose of the meeting was not to consider any proposals for reversing the fortunes of the division. Instead, her boss introduced an organizational expert to help the group with its "team dynamics," so that the group could work together in harmony, with no one rocking the boat or making the others uncomfortable. The message for Diaz came through loud and clear: good team players support one another. End of discussion. End of debate within the division. And, as it turned out, end of the division itself, which continued to hemorrhage cash until it was sold off at a distressed price.

Lastly, consider the saga of Harvey Gittler, vice president of operations for a manufacturing company, who one day refused to play the hype game when corporate management came to visit. According to Gittler, no one else was willing to make an honest assessment of the current position of the division. The head of engineering, for example, expressed enthusiasm about a new line of state-of-the-art products, without mentioning the continuing reliability problems. The head of marketing raved about the tremendous customer response, while failing to report that product returns were almost equaling shipments. And the head of sales projected tremendous growth in revenues, although the market reaction to date suggested that the forecast was grossly overstated.

Against this backdrop of defective products, a growing mountain of inventory, and unrealistic sales forecasts, Gittler tried to give a straight story when it came time to talk about the division from a manufacturing perspective. His reward? An admonishment from his boss to "change his attitude," followed by a handwritten note from his boss's boss at corporate that said, "I really can't understand your present sense of anxiety. You have a manufacturing guy's dream—a sold-out plant; a need to scale up production; a hungry, worldwide sales organization; a supportive relationship with engineering."

Gittler drew this conclusion: "There is a limit to how much one can speak out, regardless of the facts. . . . No one, especially the brass, wants to hear the truth in those settings. That's why, in my next job, I did not repeat my mistake. I told it the way 'they' wanted to hear it."

The common thread through all these examples of disloyalty tests and teamwork traps is that subtle—and not so subtle—signals of career-limiting moves have a chilling effect on the flow of information. Managers who send such signals, no matter how subtle they are, will never get the critical information fast enough (if at all), regardless of how many new approaches they try, or how much they manage by walking around, or how open they proclaim their doors to be.

In the end, limiting the risk of catastrophic losses depends primarily on whether you regard people who come to you with bad news or new ideas as liabilities or assets to you and to the organization. If you regard them as liabilities, nothing else you do matters. If, on the other hand, you regard them as assets, there are a number of techniques you can use to reinforce that message. Two among these are to offer the opportunity of anonymity where appropriate, and to avoid "treasure hunt" questions for which there is only one (already predetermined) "right" answer.

Blindfolding the Seeker

Economist Thomas Sowell has a theory about speaking up, which he states as follows: "There are only two ways of telling the complete truth—anonymously and posthumously." The corollary to Sowell's dictum is that those who want to get more of the facts need to find ways to allow those who might conceivably fear retribution to speak anonymously. Nonetheless, the advantages of anonymity are frequently overlooked or disregarded as unnecessary, often on the premise that "we all trust one another here." One company, for example, developed a comprehensive and "confidential" survey of employee concerns. But it also required respondents to record their identification numbers on their forms. At another, executives claimed that they wanted an "open environment," but would consider no employee issue that was submitted anonymously. And at a third, the CEO decided to commission a set of confidential interviews to test employee satisfaction. Whom did he plan to hire? A close family member who was experienced in this kind of work. In all three cases, some employees simply decided to tailor the information they provided in the interest of long and healthy careers.

Exit interviews also illustrate how the lack of anonymity can lead to distorted results. Many organizations use people in their personnel departments to conduct these interviews, under the theory that employees who are leaving will have nothing to hide. But quite the reverse is true, for there is frequently a "standard story" that is seen as the graceful way to leave.

At each of three professional services firms, for example, employees understood the acceptable story for leaving: at one it was the higher compensation being offered by other employers; at the second, too much travel; and at the third, unreasonable hours. At all three, many people did leave, in part, for these reasons. But there were other, more important reasons that prudent employees did not disclose, such as poor supervisors and lack of control over their work. Mindful that "you never know whose path you might cross in the future," many exiting employees are unlikely to believe promises that an interview with a company employee will be held in confidence. Without an auxiliary method to check responses—for example, an annual anonymous questionnaire to all employees who have left during the previous year, or supplemental confidential interviews—the distortion resulting from the standard story is likely to persist.

In the same way, company-conducted interviews with customers, suppliers, or distributors who are dependent on the company are unlikely to provide unbiased results. Like hospital patients being asked to evaluate medical staff that are going to be on duty the next day, these respondents are going to be unlikely to complain. When oil prices were sky-high and still climbing in the early 1980s, for example, oil companies were on allocation for the supplies they used in their exploration and development activities. In confidential interviews, the purchasing agents at these companies were outraged at the ever-increasing prices and the high rate of defects in the products being delivered. Nonetheless, most were not willing to complain publicly. (They neither forgave nor forgot, however, when the oil prices came tumbling down again later in the decade. Purchasing agents can have long memories.)

Eliminating the Treasure Hunts

Managers conduct treasure hunts every day with their employees. Here's how the game works: the manager either asks questions as a test to see if the employees can come up with the "right" opinion, or asks a leading question in which the "correct" answer is already embedded. The questions can be as trivial as the style of letters to be used in the corporate logo or as important as what investment choices to make. On the surface, such questions create the appearance of openness. But in reality, the game is made clear either by the manager's response (disappointment or irritation when the "wrong" answer is given) or by the question itself ("I'm pleased with this ad; what do you think?"). Usually the only person fooled in this game is the boss, however, since his or her subordinates will have long since learned that rather than being asked for their opinions, they are really being asked to support someone else's.

Such tactics are not new, nor are they exclusive to the business world. When Lewis Carroll wrote *Through the Looking Glass*, for example, he was unhappy with the drawing commissioned for the frontispiece and therefore conducted a nineteenth-century version of market research by writing to his target market, the mothers of young children. He sent out about thirty letters that said the following:

> "I am sending you, with this, a print of the proposed frontispiece for *Through the Looking-glass*. It has been suggested to me that it is too terrible a monster, and likely to alarm nervous and imaginative children; and that at any rate we had better begin the book with a pleasanter subject.
>
> "So I am submitting the question to a number of friends, for which purpose I have had copies of the frontispiece printed off.
>
> "We have three courses open to us:
>
> "(1) To retain it as the frontispiece.
>
> "(2) To transfer it to its proper place in the book (where the ballad occurs which it is intended to illustrate) and substitute a new frontispiece.
>
> "(3) To omit it altogether.
>
> "The last named course would be a great sacrifice of the time and trouble which the picture cost, and it would be a pity to adopt it unless it is really necessary.

"I should be grateful to have your opinion, (tested by exhibiting the picture to any children you think fit) as to which of these courses is best."

It is perhaps not surprising that the second option prevailed.

Guessing games are fun for children's parties, and leading questions are efficient for litigators, but within organizations they create obstacles to the free flow of vital information.

CREATING REWARDS

Even if you've reduced the minor costs and major risks to their theoretical minimums, you haven't done enough if the possibility for positive gain for the speaker is low or nonexistent. Sometimes the rewards that make it worthwhile to volunteer information need to be monetary; for example, participants in market-research projects are often paid for their time, and participants in gain-sharing plans are awarded a portion of the savings or profits that result from their ideas. But in many cases, those who have the information want one single thing above all: action.

Lights, Camera, Action!

The idea that action is a reward in itself seems to get lost as many companies make the pro forma effort to ask their constituencies for their ideas. But techniques such as suggestion boxes or management by walking around are unlikely to work if there isn't evidence of a working receiver at the other end. At a large electronics firm, for example, one senior manager, inspired by *In Search of Excellence*, hit the hallways to wander around and mingle with his subordinates. His approach was personal and empathetic; he remembered to ask a secretary about her son who had just begun college, an engineer about his sick mother, and a janitor about the adult education course he was taking in his spare time. Nonetheless, the technique didn't seem to be working, for he never heard new information that might help him run the company better.

The reason for this situation turned out to be simple. During each of his wanderings, this manager always asked the *same* questions of the *same* people. The wanderings had become a ritual rather than a genuine mechanism for information exchange.

Even more destructive is not acting upon or responding to the information that is offered. In fact, asking without acting is far worse than not asking at all, for it breeds cynicism. Take the company that did an internal survey, found that the greatest source of dissatisfaction concerned the cafeteria, published the results, and then . . . did nothing. Said one manager, who wished to remain anonymous: "Before, we could kid ourselves that the bosses did not know how bad the cafeteria was. After the survey, we knew they just didn't care."

Or consider the chemist who was asked to help redesign a sample compositing room. He and his colleagues agreed that a sloped floor to the drain was the most important feature to include in the renovation because then they could hose down all the raw materials quickly and efficiently. Excited about the chance to have input into the decision, they met on their own and even drew up blueprints for their proposed design. But when the dust settled, they found themselves working in an expensively remodeled room—built with a straight floor. In the absence of either explanation or action, this chemist switched off. Or as he puts it: "My enthusiasm for my company has been beat out of me. So now my enthusiasm is for me. I do a professional job. I can cover my bases. But as far as the fate of my company, as long as there is a signature on my paycheck every week, I couldn't care less—so don't tell me how they are interested in our suggestions for improvements."

But while the lack of action can generate cynicism within an organization, the expectation of action can open a floodgate of creativity. That was the experience of a company we'll call Applegate Industrial Products when it decided to experiment with an ideas program to explore new options for growth. When the company embarked on the program, one senior manager of the $200 million company scoffed that the approach would at best generate only four new ideas. Instead, 250 ideas were submitted during the first year, and more than 750 ideas in the following three.

The ideas ranged from new product and business ideas to ways to save money—everything from companies to acquire to new ways of packing pallets. More importantly, the program signaled a different way of doing business. As one executive now explains: "It was more than just the ideas, although we did get a lot of them. It was really a mechanism for cultural change. We had been a closed organization and we used this to signal that things were opening up. The message was real, and so was the change."

What was Applegate's secret? The ideas began pouring in when management understood that the primary barrier was not a lack of ideas or the need for financial rewards, but rather the belief that offering ideas was a futile gesture worth neither the time nor the effort involved. A series of confidential interviews revealed that in the past, employees believed no one listened to, or even wanted, their suggestions. One person described his boss's receptivity to new ideas this way: "When my boss says, 'I hear what you're saying,' that means 'don't bug me about this anymore.' Then I know his mind is closed."

In addition, no one seemed to know what happened to ideas after they were suggested—except that they never appeared again. "In the black hole" or "in the tunnel headed toward the black hole," was the commonly understood destination of the few ideas that people bothered to submit. So it was not surprising to find that people at Applegate also felt that there was no upside for making the effort to suggest new businesses or better ways of doing things—no credit, no atta-boys, and, worst of all, no action.

At Applegate, the key to opening the flow of information was responding to the ideas received. The company used news-letters, award ceremonies, and prizes to highlight the new ideas program. Applegate's president demonstrated top manage-ment's commitment to action by personally thanking those who submitted good ideas and then following up on their implementation. And most important of all, the company be-gan to act on the ideas that were submitted—from creating a new product line that added about 10 percent to the revenues of one of the business groups, to setting up a new operation for refurbishing product dispensers that added about half a percent to the bottom line of another.

For companies like Applegate, a structured ideas program can be an important mechanism for keeping the informal flows of information primed. And these can be designed with a va-riety of objectives in mind. In some companies, for example, such programs are used for very particular purposes so that they produce many ideas but only of a certain kind. One for-eign employee of a Japanese company, for instance, describes his company's *kaizen taien* (continuous improvement) program as one that would accept only small cost-reduction ideas. "I had a lot of ideas, but most of them I could never submit because they weren't the kind of ideas our managers wanted to consider. Still we had to submit one idea per year per section member. So we recommended that we only stamp the first page of each fax to head office, rather than every page as required. That fit the rules, and now we only stamp the first page of each fax." Granted, this company may have missed some big ideas, but it had an outstanding record of collecting and acting on hundreds of thousands of small ideas aimed at cost reduction—and year after year has achieved an advanta-geous cost position relative to its competitors.

• • •

It's hard to imagine many automotive nameplates more preeminent than Jaguar. Yet in 1980, Jaguar sold just 3,021 cars in North America. The problem was basic: the cars broke down so often that, as the old joke went, customers needed two to provide the road time of one ordinary car. As part of the company's turnaround, Jaguar's chairman and CEO, John Egan, set his sights on a reenergized dealer network. This is what he did at his 1980 sales presentation: "I met with all of the dealers and I gave them the strangest sales presentation. What I did . . . [was] to tell them in which month their favorite complaints would be solved. . . . [I said] 'Gentlemen, on the first of January [1981], Jaguar introduces its North American dealers to the round tire,' and there were roars of approval. Then I said, 'In February, the radio aerial will go up and will go down.' Another roar of approval. By the time I was finished, they said, 'If you can make cars without problems, we can break all records.' " He did, and they did. In 1981, the dealers more than tripled their volume of cars sold; by 1985, the numbers had risen to 20,528.

Sometimes it's just amazing what people will do and the information and ideas they will pass on when they know that they can make suggestions easily and without penalty and that good ideas will be recognized and rewarded with action.

THE FACTS ARE MORE LIKELY TO FLOW WHEN MANAGERS:

- Give up the idea that they have to carry only half of the burden if they want others to suggest ideas and offer concerns

- Figure out the penny-ante costs to speaking up and get rid of them

- Use anonymous formats whenever sensitive questions are asked

- Recognize when they are asking "leading questions" (and that they will likely receive censored data when they do so)

- Identify the organization's (and their own) definitions of loyalty and teamwork

- Think hard about what happened to the last five people who volunteered ideas or observations that would have required change

- Consider a structured "ideas" program

- Reward good information and ideas with recognition and action

CHAPTER FOUR

◆ ◆ ◆

We Know How to Win
in Our Business

I tell you, Wellington is a bad general, the English are bad soldiers; we will settle this matter by lunch time.

—NAPOLEON BONAPARTE,
THE MORNING OF THE BATTLE OF WATERLOO

THE ASSUMPTION:

We know how to win in our business.

THE REALITY:

The business's strategy is
mostly on autopilot.

THE RESULT:

Managers lose control
of their business's future.

SOME COMMON SIGNS WHEN
THE REAL STRATEGY IS ON AUTOPILOT

- Regardless of what the strategy says, most decisions are driven by meeting the financial goals for the next quarter.

- The company has rooms full of data, bookshelves full of analyses, and floppy disks full of files, most of which seem to have little or no relation to the actual decisions the business's managers can or do make.

- The business's plans are full of words about the "technique du jour" (quality, productivity, customer service, or whatever) without any concrete definition of what these terms mean for *this* business.

- The strategy relies heavily on what has worked in the past, even though competitive conditions have changed.

- The strategy relies heavily on what was done in the past, even if it didn't work.

- The real strategy being followed is different from the one in the plans.

- Many managers believe they would act very differently if they owned the business.

Sometimes truth is stranger than fiction, as a number of purchasers of computer components discovered when they unpacked boxes that were supposed to contain hard disks—but instead were filled with clay bricks. A practical joke? Unfortunately not. Shipping bricks instead of hard drives was just one of the many unusual tactics that some employees of MiniScribe, a California disk-drive manufacturer, used in their efforts to do whatever it took to meet the company's goals and thereby earn their bonuses. Other maneuvers included the following:

- Booking phantom sales: In one case, MiniScribe shipped $18 million worth of drives to a customer that had ordered about half that amount; by the time the excess had been returned, the higher number had already been booked as revenue. Shipments to certain warehouses were also booked as sales, even though the customers were invoiced only on receipt of the shipment from the warehouses. A former employee estimates the gap between drives booked as sales but not yet invoiced at $80 million to $100 million.

- Tossing defective drives into a storage area called the "dog pile" and booking them (as well as the returned bricks) as inventory rather than as losses in excess of the reserves for defective merchandise and bad debts: Sometimes, according to one of MiniScribe's engineers, drives from the dog pile would be reshipped to new customers. Investigators estimate that $3.5 million of the company's inventory value carried into 1988 was obsolete parts and scrap.

- Packaging contaminated disk drives so they could be booked as inventory: During the fourth quarter of 1988, the company reportedly handled approximately 6,100 drives this way.

What happened at MiniScribe was the unintended result of setting aggressive goals and then providing strong incentives for meeting them. The story is so bizarre that it is easy to dismiss it as irrelevant to any other enterprise. Yet many companies also assume that they operate with a viable strategy simply because they have set financial goals or because they have written a strategic plan.

Goals and plans are elements of creating a strategy, but in most cases neither (or even both) are sufficient for doing so. The danger is not so much in an incomplete strategy, however, as it is in the *illusion* of strategy. For many companies, the process of setting goals subtly leads to the feeling that a strategy is in place. "We have the growth numbers we want to achieve, therefore we have a strategy to grow" is the kind of thinking that takes place. Yet if the goals aren't linked to a viable strategy (but are linked to strong incentives), people may do all sorts of crazy things to meet their numbers. For others, the process of writing a plan leads to the same feeling that a strategy has been set. "We've filled out the forms and done the analyses, therefore we have a winning strategy" is the typical logic. But if the analyses are removed from the decisions that managers actually make (and if the analyses are done with a fill-in-the-blanks approach to boot), the real strategy being followed will be different than the one in the plans. In either case, the goals and the plans become *substitutes* for setting a direction based on a solid understanding of how the company can win in its industry.

There is a solution, however. It starts with understanding the limits of stretch goals and of paper plans. But its core is bringing strategy back from the stratosphere, by thinking about the strategy of an ongoing business in terms of the decisions that managers face every day: what to give the customer, at what price, and with what costs.

MANAGING BY THE NUMBERS

Setting aggressive goals has always been a popular management tool because such targets encourage people to do more than they think is possible. According to the theory, if you give people incentives and then get out of their way, they will keep achieving ever-increasing goals, allowing the company to become more effective and more productive. But numerical targets describe only the results that the company seeks to achieve. If they aren't accompanied with some feasible guidelines about how to achieve them, they will either take on a life of their own (typically when they are linked to strong incentives) or die by neglect (typically when they are not).

The Billion-Dollar Bogey

How can goals create the illusion of strategy? Consider a brief history of MiniScribe and its CEO, Q. T. Wiles. As the former chairman of Hambrecht and Quist, an investment firm that in 1985 took a $20 million position in MiniScribe, Wiles had turned the ailing drive maker into a highly successful and respected company. But in late 1986, Wiles decided he wanted to do more than nurse the company back to health—he wanted to be at the helm of a billion-dollar company.

To achieve his objective, Wiles laid out a series of stretch goals, the achievement of which became the sole criterion for payouts under the company's bonus plan. At first, Wiles's system seemed to work like a charm. As a former accountant for the company later explained, "It was just amazing to see how close they could get to the number they wanted to hit." Starting from its base of $185 million in 1986, the company grew to $362 million in 1987, then targeted an increase to $660 million for the next year.

The house of cards began to tumble when an audit revealed "massive fraud" at MiniScribe, culminating in the company's filing for Chapter 11 protection at the beginning of 1990. It doesn't appear that Wiles had any intent to defraud his customers; according to his friends, he was truly shocked by what the investigators found and believed that he had been "blindsided" by the actions of others within his firm. Nor does it appear that the financial targets were impossible to achieve through legitimate means. Though extraordinarily ambitious, the billion-dollar sales target was attainable, at least in theory: A competitor, Conner Peripherals, had only $113 million in sales in 1987 and is estimated to exceed the $1 billion mark for fiscal 1990. The difference was that at MiniScribe the link between the company's strategy and the actions taken to reach its goals had somehow come undone.

Though extreme, MiniScribe's experience is not unique. For instance, ex-employees of Dun & Bradstreet's Credit Services unit, which generates credit reports on almost ten million companies, claim that production goals led some D&B reporters either to "simply regurgitate" information supplied by the companies being investigated or, in a few cases, to estimate the missing data based on "flimsy evidence." (The company disputed their claims.) Many other companies, in industries as diverse as processed foods and high-tech weaponry, have encountered similarly unpleasant surprises.

Basing employee compensation on financial targets is nothing new, nor is it unduly risky: countless companies do it and achieve stunning results. The unacceptable risk comes when a company sets the targets without providing guidelines about its general approach for achieving them. In this case, the numbers themselves become the strategy instead of a measure of the strategy's success. The lesson is simple: If people's livelihoods and careers depend on achieving stretch goals, and they aren't given the means to do so, they will devise their own. "Bricks" come in all sizes, shapes, and forms, ranging from the real stuff in MiniScribe's case to a variety of shortcuts that run counter to successful business practices.

It Don't Mean a Thing If It Ain't Got That Swing

Managing by the numbers also doesn't work when people see the goals, the incentives, or both as so much meaningless chatter, a kind of background noise accompanying every corporate speech, memorandum, and annual report. At one high-tech company, for example, the CEO was confident that everyone in the senior management ranks understood the new goals he had set. And a series of confidential interviews showed that he was correct, they all did. There were two hidden weak spots in the understanding of these senior executives, however. The first was that most of them didn't have the faintest idea of how to translate the CEO's goals into actions, and the second was that they saw little relationship between achieving the goals and any personal benefit. In consequence, they resigned themselves to what they saw as more of the same: hard work and a subtle, but inexorable, decline in the company's performance. Which is exactly what happened until a crisis forced major change.

But even when the goals are tangible, if those who have to achieve them don't see them or the rewards associated with their achievement as desirable, odd things can happen. That was the experience of a company that tried to use a "Rude Hog" contest to discourage its service representatives from being surly with customers. The contest rules were simple: the sales rep with the lowest customer satisfaction rating for the period won the award. The only hitch was that the employees, who didn't buy into the goal, began to compete actively for the designation. Rather than being an incentive for improved service, the award became a way for the employees to express their feelings about their company.

101

In short, goals can be more or less effective depending on the incentives associated with them. But when used as a substitute for a strategy, two kinds of problems are created. If such goals are tightly linked to incentives, the purposeful and coordinated action that results is likely to backfire. If they are not, the odds of a backfire go down, but so do the odds of purposeful and coordinated action. In either case, managing by the numbers can lead to the illusion that you know how to win in your business, even when quite the reverse is true.

MANAGING BY THE BOOKS

The usual antidote to managing by the numbers is trying to manage by the books—the strategic-planning books, that is. Walk into any major U.S. company today, and you are likely to find bookshelves straining under the weight of black vinyl binders, spiral-bound consultants' reports, and boxes of floppy disks containing spreadsheets and bubble charts. In many companies, the formal strategies embodied in these reams of papers and disks provide little guidance, because the world is changing too fast for the actions detailed in them to make any sense. In addition, they are likely to be written from such an academic point of view that managers cannot translate them into day-to-day decisions. The result: despite the effort put into them, the investment in "strategy" is often wasted; the plans are either too inflexible or too abstract to provide practical guidance.

The Mirage of Sustainability

One of the problems of reliance on traditional plans is that these documents often follow the classic definition of strategy, which usually includes something about "sustainable competitive advantages." But such advantages are often fleeting, because current and would-be competitors are always striving to turn current leaders into future laggards.

Consider the fates of the "excellent companies" described in *In Search of Excellence*, published in 1982. Peters and Waterman used six criteria of financial performance, three that measured growth and three that measured returns. But for the 29 excellent companies that were still publicly traded in 1985, a comparison of statistics for 1981 to 1985 with those for 1976 to 1980 shows *negative* trends:

- Asset growth rates declined in 25 of the 29 companies.

- Equity growth rates declined in 27 of the 29.

- Market-to-book ratios declined in 20 of the 29.

- Average returns on total capital declined in 24 of the 29.

- Average returns on equity declined in 23 of the 29.

- Average returns on sales declined in 24 of the 29.

Even more interesting, a portfolio of 1980's 39 *worst* companies, based on the same criteria, outperformed the excellent companies in the 1981 to 1985 period by a significant margin. With similar betas and standard deviations, these previous poor performers beat the S&P 500 by 12 percent per year, versus 1 percent for the excellent companies.

The authors of the study explained their results in terms of a "regression to the mean"—the statistical tendency of the performance of both leaders and laggards to moderate over time and approach the average for the group. *Why* this happens in business is the more important point. One reason is that what appears to be an advantage can often be overwhelmed by competitors who create a new way to win.

Think about Formica. When most people hear that word, they think about a universally-known brand name—like

Kleenex for facial tissue or Xerox for photocopiers. The Formica brand name should therefore be a formidable competitive advantage. But chances are, if you chose a plastic laminate countertop for your new kitchen any time during the last twenty years or so, your materials came from the Ralph Wilson Plastics Company rather than from the Formica Corporation. Why? One reason is that Formica has concentrated some of its resources on expansion into non-U.S. markets. But another reason is Wilson's ability to get its products to customers faster than Formica can. With a network of 15 regional warehouses, Wilson can deliver standard laminates to its distributors in one day. And using a production process based on simplified, though more expensive, resins, it can deliver custom laminates within ten days versus, at one time, as long as 25 days for Formica. Ultimately, Wilson's ability to move faster was a greater advantage than Formica's powerful brand name.

Even when a company has an advantage that seems sustainable, the company can be vulnerable to a competitor who learns how to benefit from the advantage too. Wilkinson Sword Group Ltd., for example, did just that and gave industry leader Gillette a close shave with its own razor. Several decades ago, when Gillette invented a superior stainless steel blade, it chose not to market the new product, fearing that consumers would replace their blades less frequently. Not wanting the technology to go to waste, however, Gillette sold it to Wilkinson, a British sword manufacturer that was entering the garden-tool business. The razor-blade maker didn't see Wilkinson as a potential competitor and therefore did not restrict it from participating in the shaving market.

But Wilkinson, which produced a limited quantity of razor blades as a promotion for its new garden tools, made a startling discovery: people would do almost anything to get their hands on the remarkable shaving blades. The company eventually saw the opportunity and moved to capitalize on it with Wilkinson Sword Blades. Gillette survived the Wilkinson challenge handily but unwittingly created a new competitor.

If they can't share in your sustainable competitive advantage, you can be sure that your competitors are working hard to immobilize it. Alexander Randall, founder of the Boston Computer Exchange, compares this process to stopping an enemy convoy of armored tanks. Attacking a tank from the front is hopeless—the armored plate is too strong. The same is true for the side or back. But tanks are gas guzzlers; they get gallons to the mile rather than miles to the gallon. If you can attack the gas trucks, you can stop the tanks.

Because competitors are always devising techniques for immobilizing their opponents' tanks, plans based on the assumption of sustainable advantages often give a false sense of security. For example, think about what could happen to a company with:

- The largest and most respected sales and support network *if* a competitor introduces a product that doesn't need service in one segment. Suddenly a competitive advantage would be transformed into a fixed-cost liability, as Canon showed Xerox by inventing a copier that used a disposable cartridge for the small-copier segment of the market. Canon buyers didn't need the service, but Xerox still had to bear the cost of the network for the remainder of its customers.

- The greatest economies of scale in manufacturing *if* a competitor invents a more flexible production process. The cost advantage would become an obstacle to meeting market shifts, as Toyota showed GM in the 1970s. GM had the cost advantage of long production runs, but Toyota could set up a changeover in a few minutes versus hours for GM. In consequence, Toyota could meet customer orders faster and offer more models— both important market advantages—while avoiding the cost penalty of large inventories.

- The best relationship with the dominant channels of distribution *if* a competitor decides to sell its products through a competing channel. The original players would not be able to use the channel without alienating their current distributors, as United States Time Company demonstrated to Swiss watchmakers in the 1950s. The Swiss had an enviable position with jewelry stores, the then-dominant channel for watches. If they moved to the nontraditional channels Timex was using—drug stores and other low-end outlets—they risked losing the cooperation of the jewelers, demeaning the image of Swiss watches, and adding to the legitimacy of their new competitor.

The historic cola wars between Coke and Pepsi provide another example of how competitors can immobilize some of the power of a competitive advantage. In 1916, Coca-Cola introduced the swirled 6½-ounce bottle that became its signature. Distinctive and perfectly designed to fit the hand, Coke trademarked the bottle and used it in its advertisements. Then Pepsi (at that time a very small rival) decided to attack the icon by introducing a 12-ounce bottle for the same price as Coke's 6½-ounce package. In 1939, this radio jingle hit the air:

"Pepsi Cola hits the spot,
Twelve full ounces, that's a lot.
Twice as much for a nickel, too.
Pepsi Cola is the drink for you."

What could Coke do? Cutting price was difficult because of all the five-cent soda machines around at the time. A larger bottle also wasn't feasible—the same shape at twice the size would have fit only the biggest hands. And the company's bottlers had a billion or so of the 6½-ounce bottles on hand.

The result was that Coke kept its famous trademark bottle and Pepsi grew.

Several decades later, in the early 1970s, Pepsi returned to a similar strategy to grow once again against Coke. Despite Pepsi's previous foray, the company recognized that "The Bottle" was still one of Coke's most fearsome competitive advantages. John Sculley, then in charge of marketing at Pepsi, undertook an extended, in-home product test with 350 families to understand more about what consumers wanted and why. From Sculley's perspective, the study had an unexpected result: the determinant of consumption at home was supply at home—the more gallons of soft drinks on hand, the more each family drank. His conclusion: "The research told us that if you could get in the door, there were few limits to [Pepsi] consumption. Instead of redesigning the standard bottle, it became obvious that . . . we should launch new, larger, and more varied packaging." Once again, the strategy worked, leading to increased sales for Pepsi. As a result, over time, more and more Coke bottlers abandoned the signature bottle, once one of Coke's greatest assets.

Of course, some companies can survive with little or no change in strategy. McIlhenny Co. invented Tabasco sauce 125 years ago. The company has never changed its recipe, still picks the peppers used in its sauce by hand, and has introduced only three other Tabasco products (including "Tabasco 7-Spice Chili Recipe"). Says Paul McIlhenny, one of the approximately 90 family shareholders in the company: "We've gotten more aggressive than previously, and I think the next hundred years will see us trying even more new things."

Nevertheless, the McIlhenny Companies of the world are few and far between. For most companies, following a strategy carved in stone is a dangerous practice. The time required to write a plan that is detailed down to a gnat's eyelash is better used to test and set general strategic guidelines. Or as Robert McNamara once said, it's better to be "directionally correct than precisely wrong."

Words Into Actions

Even as statements of direction, most strategic planning efforts fail because they are chock-full of analyses and words that have ceased to have any meaning in terms of the daily decisions made within the organization.

The analyses will be familiar to anyone who has put together or read a strategic plan. Often these reams of data have important elements but are largely irrelevant to the daily decisions of even the topmost managers in the organization. At worst, they are analysis-on-autopilot, done simply because they have always been done even if they are now completely disconnected from the business of the business. Economist Thomas Sowell, for example, tells of this initial meeting with the head of the economic forecasting unit of a large corporation:

Unit manager: "Our statistical data cover all aspects of the economy and go back 30 years."

Sowell: "Then you could print tables showing all your predictions over the last 30 years—and alongside, another table showing what actually happened."

Unit manager: [after a stunned silence] "I can see that we are not going to get along."

Even more destructive is the empty verbiage that often forms the backbones of strategic plans and of the mission statements that accompany them. But empty words lead to empty plans. Here is a short list of some key offenders:

- Quality

- Employee empowerment

- Customer-driven

- Low-cost producer

- World-class

The problem? Words like these often mean nothing unless they are defined using concrete examples. Take "quality," for example. If you run a restaurant, does "quality" mean serving everyone at a table at the same time or serving each person when his or her meal is just off the stove? Or take "empowerment." Everyone wants employees to be able to make better decisions in their jobs. But "empowerment" can mean permitting employees to go over the heads of people higher than they are in the organization if they think something is wrong. Are you prepared for that kind of environment? Questions like these can be resolved, of course, but without concrete definitions, words like "quality" and "empowerment" either mean nothing or can mean something different to each person who uses them.

In contrast to using empty words like these, bringing the vocabulary of strategy to life is a never-ending task for management, as the experience of Scandinavian Airline Systems shows. Under the leadership of Jan Carlzon, SAS took on the goal of becoming the preferred airline of the business traveler, and the front line accepted the task with great enthusiasm. Yet despite the airline's new and uncontested superiority in the way everyone at SAS treated the customers, the company was surprised to find that, all things being equal, the business traveler *still* often chose other airlines.

Some digging provided an explanation of the problem. On-time performance, measured by time of push-off from the gate, is crucial to business travelers. But SAS's record for punctuality had gotten *worse* as a direct consequence of how the company's front-line employees understood what service quality meant. They had embraced their new mandate to make every effort possible to accommodate passenger needs, but they didn't understand the relative importance of on-time performance. The result? If the New York to Copenhagen flight was delayed, they would hold the Copenhagen to Stockholm flight for its connecting passengers. Similarly, if a flight was one dinner short, they would hold the plane at the gate until the remaining meal could be delivered.

Once the problem was clear, SAS could define quality more precisely while still leaving its execution in the hands of those on the front lines. Today, if the first leg of a flight is late, the connecting leg still leaves on time, and the late-arriving passengers are reticketed, even if the next flight is not SAS's. Similarly, if the full complement of flight attendants is not present or the flight is one dinner short, the plane flies with the minimum crew size or without the one dinner, and the crew does its best to reduce any inconvenience to passengers or finds a creative way to overcome it.

But if companies get rid of the empty words that clog mission statements and strategic plans, what will be left to explain to people what they should do? Try descriptions that use words with clear meanings, augmented by anecdotes, illustrations, and examples; a story with a clear rationale is worth a thousand pages of jargon. And telling stories has an additional benefit: the process of selecting appropriate stories forces managers to be very clear about exactly what the goals mean, why they were selected, and how they will be reached.

STRATEGY AND THE PRACTICAL MANAGER

Take a look at any written strategy for any organization. Chances are that you will discover a very odd thing: the plan doesn't provide real guidelines for the most common managerial decisions. For example, creating "barriers to entry," a staple of strategic plans, is undoubtedly a desirable action. But most managers don't get to their offices on Monday morning and say, "Okay, what do I need to do today to create a barrier to entry?" To the contrary, the front line of managerial decision making concerns the basics of business: delivering products that have a combination of benefits and price that the market finds attractive at advantageous costs to the company, and then figuring out how this strategic triangle of delivered benefits, price, and costs might or should change over time. Everything that most managers do most of the time should therefore be aimed at some aspect of keeping the product's (or service's) delivered benefits, price, and costs in balance with either current or anticipated customer needs and competitive realities.

Issues like "barriers to entry" still come into play, of course, because they can be used to prevent competitors from offering a particular set of benefits (as with a patent) or from achieving a certain cost position (as with scale). But any strategic plan that doesn't make the connection to "delivered benefits, price, and costs, over time" is not likely to provide real guidance for the day-to-day efforts of managers, which in turn determine the real strategy followed by the organization.

Focusing on these four variables leads to a very specific definition of strategy as: *the ongoing process of figuring out how to give a group of customers a better deal than the competition can and still make money, and continuing to do so even as the environment changes.* Even more simply put, strategy is a way of *providing the best deal profitably over time.* A simple diagram of this definition and its relationship to the strategic triangle of benefits, price, and costs is shown in Figure 4-1.

This emphasis on profitability does not mean that the *goal* of every organization should be to maximize profits, however. Nonprofits need to worry about sufficient profitability to support their cause. Japanese companies often talk about their obligations to employees, customers, and shareholders—in that order. A Danish company describes its goal as improving the way people live and work; it therefore sees profitable performance and financial security as a way to pursue new ideas without delay. For all three, profitability is essential, but as the *means* rather than the ends.

111

Figure 4-1: The Strategic Triangle

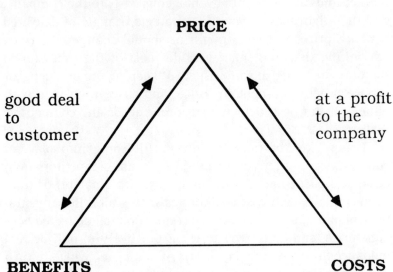

Of course, any approach that doesn't lead to superior financial returns ultimately reduces the company's ability to reach its primary goal, whatever that may be. For that reason, a good strategy for any organization requires solid thinking about delivered benefits, price, and costs, over time. Yet even in companies that spend enormous amounts of time on planning and bring in armies of consultants, assumptions about one or more of these variables are often faulty. How else can one explain companies that:

- Focus on benefits that are not highly valued by their target customers, with the result that there is a negative gap between the prices the customers are willing to pay and the prices they need to charge in order to cover their costs? (That was the problem for AT&T's

PICTUREPHONE in the 1970s. Business users loved the product—but not at the price AT&T had to charge to cover its costs.)

- Think about price without a clear understanding of competitive offerings, with the result that the competitors' products continue to win the market? (That was one of the problems for a whole string of GM's "import fighters" like the Chevette and the Vega.)

- Concentrate on costs to the exclusion of value delivered to the customer, with the result that target customers flock to competitors who charge them a little more money for a lot more value? (That was the problem for duPont's Corfam, an artificial leather intended for, but barely ever used in, the shoe business.)

- Assume that their current strategies or most recent moves will keep them in first place indefinitely, with the result that they are blindsided by competitors or new entrants who find a better way to juggle benefits, prices, and costs? (That was the problem for just about every has-been number-one company in every industry, from the *Saturday Evening Post* to the United States Steel Company. Or as Arnold Toynbee once noted, "Nothing fails like success.")

All these disasters are common, as the next two chapters show in detail. And what's more, they frequently occur to companies that think they have rigorously tested their key strategic assumptions. Preventing errors like these therefore requires different tests and different ways of testing.

Real World Strategy Tests

One way to check a strategy is to see if the following four questions have positive answers when applied to your product or service (it's no good to have positive answers to only three of the four; all four are required for a strategy that will hold together):

1. **The "Score Board" Test** is the first building block, addressing the benefits to the consumer. The test asks, "Does your product 'score' enough points from enough customers to make a potential market?"

2. **The "Good Deal" Test** adds price to the equation to determine how customers see your product in comparison to your competitors' products. Here's the question: "Does enough of your potential market evaluate the price/benefits of your product as the best deal available?"

3. **The "Bank Roll" Test** adds the third building block, costs, and indicates whether you can meet the market requirements and still make an adequate profit. The question is, "Will your cost position allow you to amass enough cash to meet your organization's goals while providing a good deal for your customers?

4. **The "Moving Targets" Test** addresses whether your answers to the first three tests will still be relevant tomorrow. It asks, "Will what you are doing today allow you to see and then adapt to changes (or create changes that are advantageous to you) in any of the first three questions?"

These four questions don't replace the tools of strategic analysis, of course. Their purpose is to provide challenges and checks, both for formal plans submitted once a year and for the managerial decisions made every day. They thereby provide a way to test the soundness not only of the written strategy but, far more important, of the actual decisions that managers make on a day-to-day basis (which may in fact bear little or no relation to what is contained in the company's mission statement or strategy books).

Real World Testing

Few management teams go through the effort of truly identifying and then challenging their implicit assumptions about
delivered benefits, prices, and costs, over time. In some cases,
this is due to a definition of team that designates one person
as the leader and everyone else as implementers whose jobs
are to do as they are told, not to question what they are told.
Or as British film director Michael Winner once explained, "A
team effort is a lot of people doing what I say."

More often, however, it's due in part to the natural process
of what Irving Janis calls "groupthink," which stifles expression of views that diverge from the *shared* expectations and
preferences of the group. As Janis explains, groupthink is
lethal because those in its sway "avoid deviating from what
appears to be group consensus; they keep silent about their
misgivings and even minimize to themselves the importance
of their doubts." Janis says that groupthink was in part responsible for the Kennedy administration's aborted Bay of Pigs
invasion; President Kennedy was more succinct, asking afterward, "How could we have been so stupid?"

Vigorous questioning of assumptions by the management
team is the key to overcoming the effects of groupthink. The
assumptions to be tested are those that, if wrong, would have
significant impact on the company's performance. Those with
which everyone on the team is in strong agreement need to
be tested periodically to ensure that the team is still playing
the right game; those with which the team is divided need to
be resolved to ensure that everyone on the team is playing the
same game. This seems like common sense, of course, except
that the process frequently does not take place.

For those who think that all this is nonsense because *their*
strategies are correct and well understood within *their* organizations, consider the findings of a 1989 survey of 611 executives at Fortune 500 companies. Eighty-two percent of the

CEOs in the sample said that they believed that the strategies they were following for their organizations were "clearly understood by everyone who needs to know." A significant number of the COOs in the same survey had a different point of view, however. Only 68 percent of them agreed with the same statement. One can only imagine what the comparable numbers would have been if people all through the organization had been asked the same question.

• • •

When Peter Harris acquired FAO Schwartz with partner Peter Morse in 1985, he uncovered a remarkable piece of inventory: the $11,000 doll house. It was quite an ordinary doll house really, one that you might expect would sell for several hundred dollars. So why was it marked at $11,000? The answer turned out to be simple: the value of obsolete inventory, rather than being written off, was being written up into the price of the doll house. While the write-ups helped managers to meet their financial targets, the practice did not serve the needs of the company.

When the $11,000 doll house was discovered, FAO Schwartz was a struggling company. Five years later it was once again a retailing star. The difference was due to a change in the business fundamentals: redefining the benefits of shopping at FAO Schwartz as a fun-filled experience, reducing the price points of some of the merchandise, and investing in infrastructure to reduce operating costs. Stretch goals and company plans are no substitute for solid strategic thinking.

USEFUL STRATEGIES ARE MORE LIKELY WHEN MANAGERS:

- Don't use numerical goals or strategic plans as substitutes for a solid understanding of how the company can win in its industry

- Link strategy and strategy analysis to managerial decisions: delivered benefits, price, and costs, over time

- Check both ongoing decisions and formal plans against the four strategy tests:

  —Score Board: Do enough consumers give your *package of delivered benefits* enough points to make a potential market for your product?

  —Good Deal: Is the *competitive price/benefits position* of your product attractive to enough consumers to make a served market of sufficient size for your product?

  —Bank Roll: Does the *competitive cost/benefits position* of your product allow you to serve this market at a profit?

  —Moving Targets: Can you move quickly to *adapt to change* (or to create change that is advantageous to you) in any of the first three questions?

- Identify those strategic assumptions that, if wrong, would have a significant impact on the company's performance

- Create forums for vigorous debate within the management team on these key strategic issues

- Periodically test these assumptions, looking for evidence to disprove them, even if everyone on the management team believes they are true

CHAPTER FIVE

————————— ✦ ✦ ✦ —————————

Of Course We Know
What Our Product Is

Nothing is as dangerous as an idea
when it is the only one you have.

—PHILOSOPHER EMILE CHARTIER

THE ASSUMPTION:

We know what the customer wants.

THE REALITY:

It's remarkably easy to deliver a set of benefits
that customers don't value highly or to miss some
that they do.

THE RESULT:

The product does less well than expected or the
company loses opportunities it could have had
(and may never even know it).

SOME COMMON SIGNS OF
MISREADING CONSUMERS

- Competitors begin to offer some products that everyone inside the company thinks are dumb (but that consumers are buying).

- People inside the company talk about what consumers "should" want and why they "should" like it.

- Target customers who buy competitors' products are dismissed as "irrational" or as not very smart.

- The people who talk about being "close to the customer" are already sure they know what the customer wants.

- The basic product concept is seen as such a self-evident truth that it has never really been questioned.

- New ideas about other ways to think about the product are rarely if ever suggested.

- Product testing focuses on a few attributes that everyone has always agreed are the most important to consumers.

- No one can really explain, using real data, the relative importance consumers assign to the various product attributes.

Profile of an Opportunity Lost

The Product: The microwave oven

The Companies: Litton Microwave Cooking Products Division and the Amana subsidiary of Raytheon's Major Appliances Group

The Promise: A new technology that would replace the kitchen oven and, to some extent, the stove-top, by making cooking faster and more energy-efficient

The Reality: A device that was great for many things and miserable for roasting meats or baking bread

The Strategy: Despite growing evidence to the contrary, stick with the concept of the microwave oven as a complete cooking device rather than thinking about it as a smaller, special-purpose appliance.

The Result: By 1986, Japanese and Korean competitors like Sharp, Matsushita (Panasonic), and Samsung walked away with the $3 billion microwave oven market that now focused primarily on ovens that could be used as "heater-uppers" and quick defrosters. Litton and Amana, by contrast, were reduced to minor players, holding a mere 12 percent of the market that they once owned.

MISREADING THE SCORE BOARD

The story of how Litton and Amana got left behind in the microwave oven wars is in part the story of two companies

123

that ultimately invested disproportionately in products that didn't match the needs of the very market they created. Since most managers think they already know what their customers want—and think they deliver it—it might be tempting to dismiss this example as an exception. But in fact, failing the score board test is remarkably easy. The most common cause of the failure? Misunderstanding the relative importance consumers place on the various attributes of a product or service.

The need to understand the implicit "decision weights" customers use when they consider a purchase is an old idea, of course, and one that successful politicians, merchants, and teachers have always known. Consider the philosophy of George Washington Plunkitt, a Tamany Hall underboss of a hundred years ago, as he explained his hold on the voters in his district:

> ". . . you must study human nature and act accordin.' You can't study human nature in books. Books is a hindrance more than anything else. . . . To learn real human nature you have to go among the people. . . . I know every man, woman and child in the Fifteenth District. . . . I know what they like and what they don't like, what they are strong at and what they are weak in, and I reach them by approachin' at the right side. . . . I don't trouble them with political arguments. I just study human nature and act accordin.''

Complicating the matter of "approachin' at the right side" for today's companies, however, is the enormous number of options consumers face and the wide variety of scoring criteria consumers use to evaluate them. The tangible elements of product design are only one part of the purchase equation, although even these can lead to an almost bewildering array of makes and models and a vast assortment of features. But, as any marketing textbook explains, the other aspects of a product to which consumers can assign decision weights include the human contact in the selling, delivery, or servicing of the goods, and the intangibles of image and reputation. With so many potential sources of product value, it's not surprising that it can be very difficult to predict and track how consumers evaluate products.

Misreading what consumers thought the product could or should be was one of the problems for the U.S. microwave oven producers. The story really begins in 1946, when scientists at Raytheon developed and patented the basic technology for microwave cooking. As U.S. consumer interest in the ovens grew during the late 1960s and early 1970s, two domestic manufacturers, Litton and Amana, dominated the market, holding a combined 75 percent share in 1973. From 1973 to 1986, demand increased rapidly, from 440,000 ovens sold per year to 12,400,000, a growth rate confirming Litton's 1978 forecast that by 1985 about half of all U.S. households would own microwave ovens.

But despite the fact that Amana's parent company had invented the technology and that both Amana and Litton had aggressively developed the U.S. market, neither company was able to capitalize fully on its discoveries. Two factors contributed to this outcome. First, when the technology was initially commercialized in the 1950s, no mass need for the ovens existed, making it difficult to anticipate the requirements of the future market and leading to subsequent cost disadvantages. Second, as the mass market in the U.S. developed two decades later, consumers slowly changed their definition of the product, making it difficult for the current leaders to notice the shift in consumer desires. Since most managers believe that they know what their consumers want, it's worth a more detailed look at how many companies end up either delivering benefits that their consumers don't value highly or missing some that they do.

When Invention Is the Mother of Necessity

Inventions often precede any apparent need. That was the case with microwave cooking technology, when a Raytheon scientist working with radar microwaves happened to notice that a candy bar in his pocket had melted. But although the technology was "made in the U.S.A.," it was sold to the Japanese. The reason: No one could imagine a need for microwave ovens in American kitchens.

The opportunity was clearer in Japan, where small kitchens without Western-style ovens made the new invention a more attractive product. Even so, the few U.S. manufacturers who recognized an export opportunity did not believe the expected returns would justify the required effort. In consequence, the Japanese manufacturers, who pushed the technology and eventually built a large market at home, were able to enter the U.S. with considerable product experience. They also had substantially lower costs, particularly in the manufacture of magnetrons (the components that generate microwaves for the ovens), which proved critical in the battle for market share.

Given the times, it's not surprising that the U.S. companies did not appreciate the implications of selling the technology for the future development of a domestic mass market. In the early 1950s, the need for fast food at home (or in the office, dorm room, or any other place microwave ovens now reside) was hardly pronounced. Few women worked outside the home, students who lived at colleges ate in school cafeterias, and popcorn was made with oil in a pot on top of the stove.

The inability to anticipate the requirements for participating in a future market when no immediate needs exist is not unique to the microwave oven industry. Consider a few of the classics:

- In 1876, Western Union refused the opportunity to buy (for $100,000) all of Alexander Graham Bell's patents

126

on the telephone, an invention the company dismissed as "an electrical toy."

- In 1897, the president of Remington Arms turned down the opportunity to buy the patent on the typewriter because, as its president said, "No mere machine can replace a reliable and honest clerk."

- In 1927, Harry M. Warner, head of Warner Brothers, initially dismissed the idea of motion pictures with sound. His view on the idea was simple: "Who the hell wants to hear actors talk?"

- In the early 1970s, almost a decade before Sony's introduction of the Walkman, top management at Zenith turned down the opportunity to continue development of a very small personal music system, because they thought the product looked like a "ridiculous toy." The initial product runs were donated to veterans' hospitals.

In all these cases, as with the U.S. microwave oven market in the 1950s, what turned out to be the future looked ridiculous at its inception.

When the Rules Change Without Notice

Even after U.S. companies became interested in microwave cooking for the home consumer and skillfully created the domestic market, another problem occurred: The consumers shifted their definition of what a microwave oven should be well before the pioneers shifted theirs.

This shift in consumers' perception of the product occurred slowly, making it even more difficult to detect. In the early phase of the market's development, producers and consumers shared the belief that the new technology could be improved

127

to the point where microwave ovens would be able to do every-thing that conventional ovens could, but faster and with lower energy costs. But even with the progress of "browning" fea-tures and the like, microwaved meats still tasted like they had been boiled, and homemade breads looked like they had been run through a dishwasher. Over time, therefore, many con-sumers largely gave up on microwave ovens for roasting and baking and began to use them for a variety of special purposes, such as thawing frozen foods, reheating leftovers, and making popcorn.

In consequence, as consumers gained a better understand-ing of the limits of the technology, *they* redefined the product concept. In their minds, the microwave oven had become a supplement to traditional kitchen ovens and ranges, not a re-placement for them, and the desired product was smaller and simpler than the complex models being touted as the wave of the future. Yet the change was obscured for the manufacturers by what they considered "common sense": What American wouldn't want a microwave oven large enough to roast a turkey or equipped with a browning feature for meats and breads?

When score board shifts like these occur, companies that do not wish to change their product strategies have to accept smaller target markets. Amana acknowledged this trade-off when it explicitly chose to limit its market by refusing to make inexpensive appliances that might compromise its image as a high-end manufacturer. On the other hand, companies that are wrongly convinced that they have remained in synch with the score board values of potential customers are likely to make disastrous investments based on overly optimistic forecasts. This was the self-made trap into which Litton apparently fell. While deeply committed to its 1978 claim that "when the pack thins out, we will be kings of the hill. . . . We do not intend to play second fiddle," Litton's forecasts of increasing sales, and therefore its investments, were still predicated to a sig-nificant extent on positioning the machine as a *complete* cook-ing device.

Why couldn't a company like Litton detect the shift? It wasn't for lack of clues. Here are just a few examples of how the press tried to sound the alarm:

- In 1978, *Mart*, a trade publication, chided the industry for its gamble on the replacement strategy. "The fact is," they wrote, "that today's customers are buying top-end microwave models to supplement their basic cooking appliances—not to replace them."

- In 1979, the *Wall Street Journal* complained that manufacturers were trying "to outglitter each other" with a variety of technological gimmicks. And, they warned, "the gadgetry overwhelms some people," including one man who commented, "You have to be Thomas Edison to know how to use it."

- In 1983, a similar theme was sounded by the publication *Merchandising Week*. Why were manufacturers still organizing cooking schools on how to cook Thanksgiving dinner in a microwave oven, they asked. From their perspective, the automatic cooking codes and cooking sensors then being introduced were missing the market by a wide margin.

- As late as the end of 1986, *Consumer Reports* noted with dismay that the latest product introductions continued to reflect the "manufacturers' persistent and possibly irrational desire to have the microwave oven replace the range."

In the end, thinking about the microwave oven as a replacement rather than as an adjunct led to poor investments. It also helped to create the opportunity for other competitors, like General Electric's new Spacemaker line, as well as Japanese and, later, Korean manufacturers that also offered smaller, simpler, and less expensive machines.

129

Missing the Point

When customers alter their scoring criteria, they vote at the cash register rather than make formal announcements. And when this change relates to the fundamental decision as to why they even buy a particular kind of product in the first place, as happened in the microwave oven industry, a company's assumption about its products can be its most dangerous piece of conventional wisdom: Armed with an incorrect product concept, the company will almost inevitably miss a large part of the market.

The microwave oven industry is not the only one to have experienced this effect, however. Consider the sophisticated U.S. investment firms that exported syndicated real estate deals to the Japanese market in the late 1980s. U.S. investors found the structure of such deals to provide a satisfactory combination of cash flow and diversification. But many Japanese investors did not value diversification as part of a real estate investment, because the Japanese concept of real estate at the time was owning a *particular* piece of property, not sharing in the proceeds of a *portfolio* of properties. Consequently, many preferred to own all of one building rather than five percent of twenty buildings, or even to own a particular room or set of rooms rather than a fixed percentage of a hotel. Predictably, the initial transfer of this instrument to the Japanese market didn't attract a stampede of buyers, owing to the gap between the scoring criteria used by U.S. investors and those used by their counterparts in Japan. Or as a Japanese officer at a major investment bank noted, one big deal was enough to fill demand for a year.

But even when there are no cultural definitions to overcome, understanding the basic "whys" of a purchase can elude even those working on familiar turf. That's what happened to Cadillac when it introduced the 1988 Allanté to the market, priced at $55,000 and targeted against the Mercedes 560L and the Jaguar X-JS. Having designed the Allanté to be the "ultimate" American two-seater luxury car, Cadillac touted the car's many accoutrements and touches of elegance, including the fact that it was shipped from Italy in a specially reconstructed 747 for its final assembly in Detroit.

From the customer's point of view, however, the advantage of shipment in a special 747 paled in comparison to the car's undergunned and unreliable V-8 engine and its poor handling, and sales lagged. Several years later, after a major redesign, the Allanté finally began to look like a car built with the target consumer's score board in mind. As one automotive expert wrote, "Having sampled the 1990 model, it's safe to say that Cadillac finally got it right. There's no more talk about air-conditioned delivery vans; now the talk is of horsepower and handling."

Of course, it's easy to use 20/20 hindsight to point out how companies have bungled golden opportunities; every company makes poor judgment calls at one time or another. But it's when an organization *persists* in making the *same* mistake that the game can be lost. And since all strategies are based on some implicit understanding of the "right" product, such persistence in misreading customer score boards can lead to elaborate plans based on weak foundations. The solution to this problem is classically simple: Test the basic product concept (even if you think you've got it), zero in on the details of the decision weights customers use in determining product value, and then periodically retest both.

JUMPING OVER THE WALLS OF OLD CONCEPTS

When a product concept is right, it provides the most efficient way to think about customer needs and keeps a company on course. But when it is wrong or applies to only a relatively small portion of the market, it can lead smart and determined managers down the wrong path. When that happens, the product concept becomes a "box" that limits a company's thinking.

Even market leaders can benefit by "breaking out of the box" and expanding their product concepts. Think about non-alcoholic carbonated beverages. If you are over 40, your product concept of soft drinks probably does not include an image of a Coke next to a sizzling-hot platter of bacon and eggs or a frosty glass of Pepsi served with sausage and pancakes. But, it turns out, many younger consumers are less likely than their parents to like coffee and tea—they gravitate toward "sweet and cold" rather than "acrid and hot." In fact, over the past ten years, morning consumption of soda has gone up nearly 50 percent. Some cola companies have redefined their product concept accordingly and begun advertising their regular products for morning consumption. One cola maker, Pepsi-Cola Company, even tested a "breakfast cola", Pepsi AM, that contains a higher dose of caffeine and bears the tag line, "the taste that beats coffee cold." Pepsi AM may not be the answer, but one thing's for sure: if you think of colas as just soft drinks, you'll miss some of the opportunity to get your product from the lunch counter to the breakfast table.

Or consider women's dress pumps. Since the early 1980s social commentators have noticed a strange sight across the nation: women "dressed for success" in expensive suits and jewelry—and sneakers. In retrospect, the market question is obvious: Why would women who obviously take great pride in their appearance allow their self-image to stop at their ankles? Some may have donned their running shoes to avoid scuffing their dress pumps on the tricky cobblestones and sidewalks of older cities. But the more likely reason is that dress pumps are very uncomfortable for certain common activities, such as walking.

To fill the need, in 1987 U.S. Shoe launched the Easy Spirit Dress Shoe line, with a claim never before heard in the shoe departments of America: "looks like a pump, feels like a sneaker." These shoes are not only easy on women's feet, they're easy on their pocketbooks as well, costing a third of the price of high-end imported models that some women wore in the effort to combine fashion and comfort. As one Easy Spirit convert explained, "For the first time, I can walk ten blocks to a business lunch without freaking out."

While U.S. Shoe's performance in some other areas has been troubled, its Easy Spirit line has been wildly successful, with a 200 percent growth rate for the two years after its introduction. The line succeeded because it expanded the concept of what a woman's dress pump could—and should—be, by defining high heels as "walking shoes" rather than as "fashion accessories." Though in retrospect it may seem obvious that shoes should be made for walking, in this case it was a revolution. As Easy Spirit proved, it all comes down to freeing the mind of self-imposed product categories and definitions.

The wall created by current product concepts can be scaled in a number of ways. Sometimes it's a matter of being receptive to unconventional ideas from unconventional sources, such as psychologists and anthropologists. Other times, it's a matter of creating situations that allow customers and company insiders to dream or explore new options. But in all cases, the essence of the process is in encouraging off-the-wall ideas and then asking, why not?

Finding Sources Outside the Box

People who are "outside the box" of typical business thinking—anthropologists, psychologists, industrial designers, or even neurologists—can be invaluable in redefining what the right product is. Applying anthropological thinking to market segments, for example, can be useful because segments often have norms that distinguish them from other segments, just as different tribes do. Tambrands, for example, was surprised at college students' negative response to a proposed ad for its First Response pregnancy test. The text of the ad went something like this:

Man: "So which is it, yes or no?"
Woman: "Now, why do you think I'm smiling?"

The implication of the ad was that the test was positive, hence the woman's smile—but for many students, a positive result on a pregnancy test is not cause for celebration. Tambrands changed the ad to say, "Until you know, nothing else matters."

Or what about using psychologists to determine not just how consumers react to certain products, but *why* they react as they do? Understanding such beliefs can be critical to a product's success, as a company that developed a better bug spray discovered. The effectiveness of the spray came from the delayed-action properties of the product: because the compound was lethal but did not kill the bugs on contact, its effect multiplied as each contaminated bug infected others. Despite its greater effectiveness, the product did not sell well. Why? One reason was that if the customers didn't *see* the bugs die, they weren't sure that the product really worked. Psychological research at a second bug-killer company provided another possible reason, however: Customers saw the bugs as their enemy and *wanted* to see them die. No dead bugs, no repeat sale.

Or what about using an industrial designer to test "inviolable" constraints in a product's design? For years, the belief within Corning Inc. was that people do not like to move pots from the stovetop to the tabletop. Davin Stowell, president of Smart Design, discovered that lifestyles have changed and, given a "pot" of acceptable aesthetics, customers would welcome the chance to move one vessel from the freezer to the microwave oven to the table. Whether called a dish or a pot, the resulting product designed by the Smart Design team is now a best-selling product in Corning's line.

134

Finally, what about using neurologists to map new connections between products and the world? Dr. Alan R. Hirsch, a neurologist and psychiatrist at the Smell and Taste Treatment and Research Foundation, has been testing the effects of odors on consumers' attitudes on spending. His results show that certain smells increase the sell. Or as Dr. Hirsch says, "Odors will be the marketing tool of the 90s. The easiest way to impact emotions is through smell." (For the record, according to Hirsch the scent women like best is the smell of flowers, whereas for men it is the fragrance of a backyard barbecue).

The purpose of using outsiders in this way is not just to provide new answers to old questions. After all, the creativity required to generate good solutions usually already exists internally. But sometimes outsiders are needed to shake up the old rules so that new ideas can be generated—and new questions asked.

Freeing Up Those Inside the Box

Product concepts can be difficult to test. Buyers and producers are likely to respond only within the box of "what is today" unless you find some way to make it easy for them to start at ground zero, so they can think about "what could be tomorrow" unfettered by their own preconceptions.

One way is just to experiment repeatedly in all possible ways; being willing to try something and then quickly using the resulting learning is a powerful form of market research. Many Japanese firms, for example, introduce vast numbers of products at home and then take the survivors abroad. In the fight for the microwave oven market, this experimentation ultimately overwhelmed the advantage that Litton thought it had when in 1982 its vice president of marketing declared, "Domestic firms can do a superior job in marketing and understanding the consumer, so [we] are not under any handicap."

Another way to break out of the box is simply to learn about consumers in the same way anthropologists approach their subjects: observe a small number of people intensively over a long period of time. When Toyota was developing the Lexus, for example, a team of Toyota engineers from Japan rented a house in Laguna Beach, California, and spent a month looking at how their neighbors lived. Nissan Motor Corporation took this approach one step further. Through the Japanese American Cultural Center, a Nissan employee, Takahashi Morimoto, spent six months living with a Costa Mesa, California, family. As Makota Tachikawa, Nissan's director of product strategy, explains, "The important thing is to get inside people's heads. Sometimes they cannot say for themselves. So we are judges, carefully watching." (There are some perils to this method, however. The family Morimoto observed has claimed that they did not know the true intention of their guest was market research and have filed suit against Morimoto, Tachikawa, and the company.)

The standard ways of asking consumers directly about what a product should or could be—focus groups and one-on-one interviews—still often provide the best combination of research and speed. Just asking an open-ended question is sometimes all that's needed, as GTE Corp. found. The company had been very confident that it was running, in today's jargon, a "customer-driven" organization. Its rigorous periodic testing showed that its telephone customers were highly satisfied with the appearance of the company's employees and with the range of services available. But in 1984, the company undertook a new approach: focus groups and personal interviews. Invited to direct the conversation rather than being asked to respond to predetermined categories, the customers revealed that their primary concerns—maintenance hours, reliability in transmission quality, and speed in emergency situations—

weren't even being tested. The difference was between asking a structured question like "Are you satisfied with the range of services we offer?" and asking an unstructured one like "Have you ever been unhappy with us or the services we provide to you? Tell me a little about when that happened and what you would like to see changed."

At other times, however, even these methods are sabotaged by questions that beg to be answered with conventional wisdom. If you had asked women about dress pumps in 1986, most would likely have talked about styling and durability. But if you had chosen a truly oddball question, like asking them to imagine that their feet could talk and having their feet respond to the question, you might have gotten a very different response—one about pain and contortions rather than lines and elegance.

Whatever the method used, the key is to find ways to think about old ideas in new ways by relaxing the current assumptions about what consumers want and why. When should such methods be applied? One obvious time is at the beginning of a product's life. And after that they should be applied again periodically, to ensure that the accumulation of both experience and quantitative research methods (such as those described in the next section) doesn't lead to an ossified product concept when there is the potential for change in the marketplace.

DETAILING THE DECISION WEIGHTS

Testing the basic product concept is only half of figuring out what consumers do (or could) want. The other half is being more precise about the scoring criteria customers use as they evaluate the many attributes of any product. The dilemma faced by higher-priced clothesmakers illustrates the importance of understanding how consumers make trade-offs. Confronted with higher costs, some, according to *The Wall Street*

Journal, have chosen to focus more on "designer names, new fabric colors or proprietary prints than on workmanship," implicitly assuming that these attributes are more important to their target customers than durability. The result? An increase in split seams, lost buttons, unraveled hems, puckered collars, and misplaced armholes.

This assumption, which may be incorrect for the U.S. market, is clearly incorrect for consumers in Japan. When designer apparel is exported to Japan, up to 30 percent doesn't meet Japanese quality standards. Often the seams are restitched by Japanese marketers of the clothing and then inspected again by store employees. Or, as an official at a Japanese apparel maker explained after rejecting one such item because the stitching holes showed along the seam when he stretched the fabric, Japanese consumers "expect high-quality items to include hidden effort, even in areas that don't show. Whether that's really necessary is a different matter."

Trade-offs like the one between stitching and styling are at the heart of every product decision, for both those who create the product and those who consider buying it. But getting consumers to explain the real decision weights they use is difficult simply because people are often not aware of the weights they place on each attribute of a product as they make a purchase decision. A better way is to let them show you *how* they make such decisions, by using a technique called conjoint (or trade-off) analysis. This technique asks customers to rank a group of products, each "composed" of a set of attributes that are varied in a systematic way, in order of likelihood of purchase. Their choices then can be analyzed to show the relative importance consumers place on each attribute in the test.

A laptop-computer manufacturer, for example, might be interested in the relative weights consumers place on the following: the display seen on the computer's monitor (backlit or nonbacklit); the machine's processing speed (8 MHz, 12 MHz, or 16 MHz); the power source used (AC power only or AC power plus battery); and the storage media (floppy disk only, hard disk only, or hard and floppy disks). The manufacturer knows that, holding aside heaviness, just about everyone would prefer a machine with a backlit display, 16 MHz processing speed, battery as well as AC power, and both hard and floppy disks. What he needs to know, however, is *which* of these are more important to what type of consumers, *and by how much*. To find out using the conjoint technique, he would give consumers a series of choices, four of which might look like the following:

Computer 394
  Backlit display
  8 MHz processing speed
  Battery as well as AC power
  Hard disk only

Computer 742
  Nonbacklit display
  16 MHz processing speed
  AC power only
  Floppy disk only

Computer 273
  Nonbacklit display
  12 MHz processing speed
  Battery as well as AC power
  Hard and floppy disks

Computer 581
  Backlit display
  12 MHz processing speed
  AC power only
  Hard disk only

How many variables a company looks at depends on the question it is trying to answer, of course. An airline, for example, considering its intercontinental route structure and plane configurations, might want to know whether such benefits as nonstop flights, superior on-time performance, or convenient scheduling are more important to the company's target market than superior service or other in-cabin amenities. In this case, consumers could be asked to rate a series of choices among which might be the following two:

139

Characteristic	Option 1	Option 2
Number of stops	1	Nonstop
Seat size (% of average)	115%	100%
Percentage of seats filled	50%	90%
On-time record	Poor	Good
Customer service rating	Outstanding	Poor
Number of movies shown	2	1
Convenience of departure time	Within three hours of target	Within 90 minutes of target

Using regression analysis, researchers can "decompose" the responses from studies like these into the component decision weights that consumers use when they make a purchase. Why bother with all of this? The advantage is that in many cases conjoint analysis provides far better data than asking consumers to tell how they make decisions. First, it reduces the risk that the respondents say something different from what they normally do, either as part of a deliberate misrepresentation or, more typically, because the true decision process is sufficiently intuitive that they are not aware of the real weights they use. Second, it tends to be more fun for the respondents than trying to explain which factors figure into a purchase decision—an important plus, because when respondents become bored, their answers to questions are less reliable. And, most important, it gets at the trade-offs that customers make when they are choosing among products or services.

140

In sum, understanding the consumers' trade-offs is essential, simply because companies have to make trade-offs in the design of any product or service, just as consumers do in their purchases, and guessing wrong is an expensive proposition. Consider one of the all-time classics in misunderstanding the consumer's trade-offs: the IBM PCjr™. Where did IBM go wrong? First was the keyboard, dubbed "chiclet" style because the keys looked like the little sugar-coated chewing gum pieces popular in the 1950s. That the keyboard was so inadequate was particularly surprising given that, as marketing consultant Milind Lele puts it, "[IBM's] Selectric keyboard was the standard for comfort and operator convenience." And then there was the matter of the storage media chosen: the PCjr used program cartridges, leading to compatibility problems. Decisions like these reflected *IBM's* design trade-offs that, in this case, did not match with the purchase trade-offs made by *consumers*. Partly because of this misunderstanding of the decision weights used by their target market, IBM had to write off the model, resulting in both financial losses as well as embarrassment in the marketplace.

• • •

Rolex watches are precision-engineered jeweled movement instruments, with retail prices that begin in four figures. Yet the accuracy of a Rolex comes close to (but neither equals nor exceeds) that of quartz timepieces selling for a fraction of the price. So why do Rolexes continue to sell? Andre Heiniger, managing director of Rolex, knows the answer. At a dinner party, someone once asked Heiniger, "How's the watch industry?" Heiniger's response: "Rolex is not in the watch business. We are in the luxury business."

It pays to know what you are selling.

THE PRODUCT IS MORE
LIKELY TO BE RIGHT
WHEN MANAGERS:

- Periodically engage in "out of the box" thinking on basic product concepts or new inventions
  —within the company
  —with customers
  —with outsiders (especially those
    with unusual perspectives)

- Periodically test the "decision weights" consumers use to evaluate products in this product category

- Actively seek data that suggest how consumers might be changing the product concept

- Do quick tests and experiments so they can lead, rather than follow, changes in the consumers' score board

- Keep a close eye on the quick tests and experiments of your competitors, and on consumers' reactions to them

- Assume that "dumb" choices by consumers send valid messages

CHAPTER SIX

◆ ◆ ◆

We Know How to
Make a Buck

*You can have any color you want, boys,
as long as it's black.*

—HENRY FORD ON HOW TO MAKE A BUCK
(HE WAS WRONG)

THE ASSUMPTION:

We know how to make a buck.

THE REALITY:

Many managers don't have a clear idea about the economic equation for providing the best deal profitably to their target market.

THE RESULT:

The company experiences unexpected losses of share or margin (or both).

144

SOME COMMON SIGNS WHEN THE ECONOMIC EQUATION IS NOT WELL UNDERSTOOD

- The product is inexplicably losing market share.

- The product is losing share but this is attributed to the inevitable result of new competition.

- People inside the company believe competitors' pricing strategies are "irrational" and that these competitors must be losing money.

- Prices are cut drastically to stem share losses (but the company can't make money at the new prices).

- Prices are raised because everyone believes that the costs are already to the bone (or doesn't want to go through the work of cutting costs).

- Cost cutting is ordered using the "cheese slicer" approach (the cuts are distributed evenly across all departments because this is "the only fair way").

- No one can give a good explanation for why a competitor seems to be making so much money.

On November 27, 1948, two employees of a fledgling company readied their display in a little alcove of Boston's Jordan Marsh department store. Back at corporate headquarters in a converted warehouse in East Cambridge, everyone wondered whether the two could sell their stock of 56 "Polaroid Land Camera Model 95s" by Christmas. One source of concern was the camera's price: $95. Nervous that the price was too high, at the last minute company executives lowered it to $89.75, still a substantial premium over the Kodak Baby Brownie, a reliable aim-and-shoot camera that retailed for just $2.75.

As it turns out, the price adjustment was totally unnecessary. Within minutes after the first instant image appeared, a mob had gathered in the store's cramped camera department, with people prepared to commit mayhem in order to walk out with one of the new devices tucked under their arms. Asked by the store's assistant manager to return the next morning, the two explained that they could arrive no earlier than 2 p.m.—the 56 cameras that had been sold were the company's entire inventory, and they had just telephoned the people in East Cambridge to speed up production. And so began Polaroid's phenomenal entry into the photography market.

Nearly 40 years later, the company staged another memorable product launch, this time for Spectra, its newest instant camera and film system. The event was held at the Century Plaza Hotel in Los Angeles with all the fanfare of a major movie opening, complete with blaring music, twirling dancers, and a two-story replica of the new camera. But there was a striking difference in outcomes between the Model 95 of 1948 and the Spectra of 1986. The Model 95 cost consumers 33 times as much as the most popular amateur camera then on the market, was launched for a song, and created a sensation. The highly advanced Spectra was priced at parity with inexpensive 35-millimeter cameras and was launched with great panache, yet fell short of expectations. What happened?

147

A GOOD DEAL IS HARD TO FIND

Emerson was right: Build a better mousetrap and the world really will beat a path to your door. There's one catch, however: the price/benefits profile of your mousetrap relative to other competing mousetraps must lead the target consumers to evaluate it as a good deal. And, as many inventors and executives have learned, a better mousetrap and a better deal are not necessarily the same thing.

Worth a Thousand Words: Model 95 of 1948; Spectra of 1986

In 1948, Edwin Land truly did invent a product that consumers saw as a good deal—even a great deal. There was nothing else like the Model 95 on the market. As an amateur camera, it greatly simplified the photographic chores of choosing the right apertures and shutter speeds. And it provided a benefit that, while previously unimaginable, was immediately attractive to consumers: instant photographs.

But the situation with Spectra was very different. Polaroid reportedly introduced Spectra in response to a shrinking market for instant cameras and film. Priced at $225 and targeted at a more affluent and sophisticated market than the company was then reaching, the product was described by Polaroid as able to produce photographs "comparable in quality to [those] taken with inexpensive 35-millimeter cameras." Backing this claim, according to Polaroid executives, was five years of market research and an advertising budget of $30 million to $40 million for the first year alone. Explained Polaroid's chairman, William J. McCune: "We felt it was worth the effort to make a major restatement of instant photography and to reposition instant photography in the eyes of the consumer."

148

Industry pundits, however, were not impressed. "The first Polaroid was magic," said the publisher of *Modern Photography* magazine, Herbert Keppler. "But the system hasn't changed very much. There isn't anything that makes this a major breakthrough for the consumer." The *New York Times* griped, "The cost of the film, more than $1 a shot, remains a drawback," noting that with the rapid expansion of one-hour processing, traditional photography had become almost instant. The *Boston Globe* warned that "Spectra is competing with many Japanese 35 mm cameras having a similar price tag yet superior optics . . . [and] lenses that are much faster." And, *Business Week* added, 35-millimeter cameras continued to have the advantage of delivering "higher quality prints at about half the price." These early reviews were prophetic. Despite Spectra's many advantages, it did not achieve the company's goal of "repositioning instant photography in the eyes of the consumer." Spectra was a wonderful camera, elegantly designed and a pleasure to use; relative to other instant cameras, there was nothing that could compare to it. But relative to the market for "fun photography," which included easy-to-use 35-millimeter cameras, Spectra was up against tough competition that was getting ever tougher.

The Economic Equation for "A Good Deal at a Profit"

Companies frequently overestimate the potential market for their new products. Many invent mousetraps that are truly better but find that they cannot price them high enough to cover the total costs of the product, yet low enough to attract buyers. And while it's obvious that price and cost are the drivers of providing a good deal profitably, frequently either the price part of the equation or the cost part is overlooked.

How does this happen? On the price side, one of two illusions typically comes into play: that the lower-cost alternatives don't deliver enough value to the consumer, or that the higher-cost alternatives charge consumers too much for what they get. Both illusions stem from not understanding the "good deal test" from the *consumer's* perspective. And both have a lethal result: They allow competitors to build markets at the expense of those who hold the illusions.

PRICE ILLUSION #1:
"CUSTOMERS DON'T WANT THAT JUNK"

Competitors who operate at the low end of a market are easy to ignore. Many managers, proud of the products their companies make, can't fathom why anyone would want something less than they offer, even if the price of the alternatives is substantially lower. Companies undone by this kind of pride may already be in the market and open to attack by new low-end products, or they may be new entrants with plans to unseat current competitors by offering what they perceive as a lot more in benefits for a little more in price. In either case, it's dangerous to dismiss less expensive products as "junk" without understanding the consumer's evaluation of these same products.

Pride Goeth Before a Fall:
"Their Product Will Fail Because It Offers Too Little"

Cuisinart was blinded by this kind of pride when competitors developed simpler, less expensive food processors. The saga began in 1984 when Sunbeam undertook a study of food-processor owners and found that half of the units bought simply collected dust—people felt the machines were too big, too complicated, too hard to clean, or a combination of all three. Based on this information, Sunbeam designed the "OSKAR"

(Outstanding Superior Kitchen All Rounder), which measured half the size of Cuisinart's standard model and sold for as little as $60—one-third the price of a basic Cuisinart. Carl Sontheimer, Cuisinart's inventor and founder, wrote off the OSKAR (which some scorned as a "gumball machine") as a joke. But Sunbeam had the last laugh when it sold 750,000 OSKARs in 1985, constrained only by its manufacturing capacity. In 1986, Sunbeam ramped up production and sold 1,400,000 of its "gumball machines." Several years later Cuisinart finally took OSKAR as a serious threat and introduced its own pint-sized model. But by then it was too late for Cuisinart to take a big piece of this new market. In 1989, after several changes in ownership and a series of other problems, Cuisinart filed for bankruptcy.

Or consider how the United States Time company unseated the market hold of Swiss watchmakers with its new product, the Timex watch. It would have been easy to write off Timex as junk. It wasn't sold at jewelry shops, but at drugstores, variety stores, grocery stores, hardware stores—just about everywhere one wouldn't expect a "real" watch to be sold. It wasn't created by craftsmen but assembled by unskilled laborers. It couldn't be cleaned or repaired; if it broke after its one-year warranty expired, the watch had to be thrown away. Yet by 1962, 13 years after their introduction, Timex watches held 30 percent of the U.S. market, a number which grew to 45 percent by 1973. Why? Take a look at industry prices in 1949. At $6.95 to $7.95, about one-tenth the price of a good Swiss watch, a Timex was in fact a very good deal for a large portion of the watch-buying market.

Techno-Visions: "Our Product Will Succeed Because It Offers So Much More"

Companies that set out to invent new and better products are particularly susceptible to underestimating the value of existing, lower-priced products. When the new product is based on a new technology, the temptation to see it as the next "Model 95" is especially strong. But this inclination is also likely to be incorrect: according to Steven Schnaars, a marketing professor at Baruch College, only 20 to 25 percent of high-growth forecasts based on new technologies are anywhere close to accurate. Here are a few of Schnaars's examples of how sexy technologies seduce companies into believing that they're offering a good deal when in fact they aren't.

- In 1970, Westinghouse introduced the "cool top" range, a cooking appliance that, using an oscillating magnetic circuit to excite food molecules, could heat food while keeping everything else with which it came into contact cool. *Fortune* magazine thought the device noteworthy enough to spotlight it in a special article on new products by Fortune 500 companies. But though the "cool top" could excite molecules, it couldn't excite consumers; the ranges cost substantially more than the conventional units and could be used only with cast-iron or steel pots. The advantages of being cool weren't sufficient to justify the price disadvantage.

- In 1972, CBS projected that systems with four speakers would replace conventional stereo "at an even faster rate than conversion [from mono] to stereo," forecasting that the market would increase to 1,000,000 units in 1973 and to 3,000,000 units in 1974. The revolution did not take place: few consumers found the sound enough improved to justify the investment in additional speakers; quadraphonic recordings were hard to find; and arranging rooms to accommodate *four* strategically placed speakers was no easy task. The incremental value to the consumer was less than the incremental price.

- In 1983, the five-year forecast for the videotex industry estimated that the increase in consumers seeking home computer-based services such as electronic shopping and banking would result in the installed base of 5,000 terminals growing to 1,900,000 by 1988. Many companies rushed to get into the market early, including AT&T, Bank of America, CBS, Chemical Bank, Citicorp, IBM, Knight-Ridder Newspapers, NYNEX, RCA, Sears, Time Inc., and the Times-Mirror Company. But by late 1987, it was clear that most consumers didn't regard the services provided as worth the price of the required hardware. Some consumers even had trouble justifying the prices of the services alone. Or as one writer in the *New York Times* then commented, "People still prefer touching the merchandise in a department store to ordering by computer, and reading a newspaper to scanning a video display tube with their morning coffee."

In all of the preceding cases, the problem was that, from the perspective of the vast majority of the potential market, the lower-priced, lower-tech alternatives *did* provide a more attractive set of benefits for the money than the new higher-priced innovation did. The companies had misread how their target consumers evaluated their existing low-cost options relative to the "better" mousetrap.

PRICE ILLUSION #2:
"CUSTOMERS WON'T PAY THAT MUCH"

The second assumption that can lead to poor pricing decisions is that "consumers won't pay that much," again an assumption that is likely to be incorrect if it is based on a rule of thumb and not on a true understanding of the consumer's definition of a good deal. When the more expensive product has benefits to which consumers attach high value but that the company ignores or discounts, this illusion will take one of two forms. The first is underestimation of the market for a new high-end innovation (usually someone else's) on the basis that customers will not buy it because its price is too high. The second is overestimation of the market for a new low-end innovation (usually one's own) on the basis that customers will flock to it because its price is so reasonable.

Misestimated Price Elasticities: "Their Product Will Fail Because Its Price Is So High"

Price elasticities make great graphs for economics textbooks, but in the real world it can be difficult to predict beforehand how much of a price premium some innovations can fetch. Who would have thought, for example, that an amateur camera priced at 33 times the most popular alternative would have had a large market—yet the first Polaroid created a whole new industry. Or that a new spreadsheet program could be sold for twice the price of the market leader—which is exactly what Lotus 1-2-3 did to VisiCalc, the creator of electronic spreadsheets. Or that a new vodka, a product that by law cannot have any distinctive taste, color, or odor, could carry a significantly higher price than nonpremium vodkas on the basis of a prestigious brand name, a distinctive bottle, and an aggressive advertising campaign. (The vodka is Tanqueray Sterling, the bottle is frosted glass with silver details, and the campaign budget is pegged at $20 million. The verdict is still out on whether the strategy will succeed.)

The same question might have been asked about compact discs for stereo sound systems. Some people believed that the market would go nowhere, because in addition to requiring new hardware, the CDs themselves were far more expensive than standard LPs. The compact disc market has grown, however, as consumers have decided that the sound quality, durability, and convenience of the new technology is worth the higher price. By 1990, LP records accounted for less than 4 percent of recording-industry sales. "There's an entire generation that has never owned a turntable," comments David J. Steffen, senior vice president for sales and distribution at A&M records.

Finally, consider some of the initial prognostications about Cuisinart in the years before Sunbeam launched the OSKAR. In fact, if he had listened to the experts, Sontheimer would have given up shortly after he began. Having introduced his invention at the National Housewares Show in 1973, Sontheimer tried to sell his device, with a retail price of $175 per unit, to buyers for upscale department stores. To say the effort wasn't successful would be an understatement; when told the price, some buyers laughed so hard that tears welled up in their eyes. That year, Cuisinart's total revenues were a few hundred thousand dollars, hardly enough to sustain the company.

The turning point occurred shortly thereafter, however, when a review in *Gourmet* magazine, calling the device "indispensable," was able to explain clearly *why* the new device was worth the money. Armed with the added credibility of similar praise from cooking celebrities like Julia Child and James Beard, the company could barely keep up with demand. What to do next? By 1979, with competing machines selling at far less than Cuisinart's standard model, Sontheimer added an even more powerful model to the line and priced it at $275. That model too was an immediate success.

Why was the premium-priced Cuisinart regarded as a good deal in 1975, and as a poor deal ten years later? One reason was that the early buyers of food processors tended to be serious cooks; for them, complexity and power were well worth the price. The later buyers, on the other hand, were looking for less and had more options, so they didn't need to even consider the high-priced products. In sum, whether the item is food processors or compact discs, the question of how much more consumers will pay for a "new and better" product depends entirely on their assessment of the value of the incremental benefits versus those delivered by the existing products. Dismissing a competitive product solely on the basis that it carries a high price is therefore a dangerous (though very common) assumption.

The Case of the Missing Benefits: "Our Product Will Succeed Because Its Price Is So Low"

The common corollary to the assumption that a high price won't make a market is that a low price will take the market by storm. Yet this assumption also will be incorrect if the new, lower-priced product does not offer those benefits that its target buyers see as essential.

How do companies end up not considering important benefits of competing higher-priced products? The problem is common when some of these benefits are "soft" in nature and therefore less easily quantified. That's what happened to a communications company that made plans to enter the video-teleconferencing field, a market that has developed much more slowly than anticipated. But you would never have guessed this, given the bullish forecast that the company used to support the necessary investments.

This was the basic reasoning: Video-teleconferencing will be a viable alternative to all in-person meetings for which the travel requirements are 500 miles or more, because it will be cheaper than the airfare, hotel, and meals of long-distance travel. And since this potential market is huge, "all" that is needed is a 1 or 2 percent share, which will lead to immense profitability.

Unfortunately, this forecast did not measure—or even adequately characterize—any of the other criteria that would go into the purchase decision. Left out were such variables as the ability to have sidebar conversations or other off-the-record interactions; the value of dropping in and seeing other people with whom formal meetings have not been scheduled; the belief that only in-person contact can provide a truly effective "glue" between people; and the reality that travel is often seen as an important job benefit.

As one observer to the process mused, "Here were all these strategic types and yet even though they also had heavy travel schedules, they couldn't make themselves think through the obvious reasons why in-person meetings are often seen as the only reasonable alternative." The glitter of the technology had overwhelmed the prosaic questions about the value consumers placed on those aspects of meetings that could not be delivered via video-teleconferencing. The result was that the company's executives badly overestimated the value of their product and therefore the prices they could charge. They thought that as long as it was cheaper than long-distance travel, they had a winner. Taking into account the attributes that the service couldn't offer, however, the prices had to be far lower still to offer an attractive alternative to in-person meetings.

Other times, however, the problem is not so much that the benefits of the higher-end products are overlooked as that they are underestimated. This was the mistake that RCA made when in 1981 it introduced the videodisc player in competition with the then-emerging VCR technology.

Like the VCR, the videodisc player was a machine that allowed prerecorded materials to be viewed on a television screen. At its inception, the RCA system had important advantages: a videodisc player was significantly cheaper than a VCR, the discs themselves were less expensive than VCR tapes, and the system was less complicated to operate while providing sharper, clearer images with better sound. But it also had one

157

important drawback: unlike a VCR, it could not also be used as a recording device.

RCA apparently underestimated the value of being able to record programs and reuse the disc. So although the initial price of the videodisc system was lower than that of the VCR, again it wasn't low enough to compensate for this drawback. And over time, a vicious cycle emerged that destroyed even this price advantage: as the VCR market grew, the price of the VCR hardware went down faster than RCA had predicted. In addition, a rental market for movie tapes developed, effectively making the tapes cheaper than the discs on a usage basis. When RCA bailed out of the market in 1984, the company's total loss was on the order of $580 million.

THE PRICE IS RIGHT

Making pricing decisions based on old rules of thumb or on the basis of untested beliefs can be dangerous business. The task instead is to understand how consumers decide what's a good deal—and what isn't. That was the difference between microwave ovens and cool-top ranges; between VCRs and videodiscs; and between Polaroid's Model 95 and Polaroid's Spectra.

Let X = Benefits and Y = Price

What does it take to understand the consumer's perspective on what is a good deal, and what isn't, for a particular market? If you like to think in terms of pictures, a market can—at least in theory—be summarized by a graph with the consumer's evaluation of the total benefits of each product expressed as a number or a score on the x-axis and the price of each product by the appropriate number on the y-axis. Each product then becomes a point on the graph, and all the points together create a pattern that tells something about how much more customers are willing to pay to get more benefits (see Figure 6-1 for an example). The shape of this curve will vary by industry: for a commodity product like steel, the ability to increase prices for additional benefits is low, resulting in a relatively flat curve; for a consumer good like automobiles, the incremental price that can be realized for additional benefits is higher, resulting in a steeper curve.

Whether or not you have an urge to grab a quadrille pad, however, the key point is that determining whether consumers see your product as providing a good deal requires looking at the benefits and prices of a broad range of competitive products. And graphs aside, on a practical level, the market does send clear signals when one product is "off the curve"—the company begins to experience losses or gains in share that it neither planned nor can explain. Obviously, companies often and appropriately price low to gain share or price high to maximize per unit margins. These movements along the curve are expected and are not the problem. The problem is share gains or losses that are *not* expected. Unexplained share losses suggest products that are overpriced relative to the price/benefit profiles offered by competitors. Similarly, unexplained share gains indicate untapped pricing opportunities.

For example, for years, conventional wisdom suggested that luxury carmakers should never drop their prices, as much to avoid damaging their image as to retain margins. But in 1989, in response to share losses in the U.S., Porsche rolled back its prices on several U.S. models by 6 to 9 percent. Said Porsche CEO Heinz Branitzki: "There's definitely an unwritten rule that says it makes no sense to lower prices, but I felt strongly that this time the rule needed to be broken." He was right; data from the market are more pertinent than old rules of thumb.

Identifying the price/benefit profiles of competing products and the market sizes associated with each is a difficult analysis,

Figure 6-1   An example of price/delivered benefits analysis

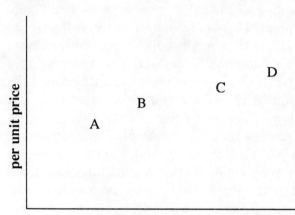

In this simple example, industry prices and benefits are pretty much in equilibrium, so there typically would not be unexplained share movements. But consider what would happen if competitor A changed its strategy and a new competitor, E, also entered at a lower price than expected, as shown below.

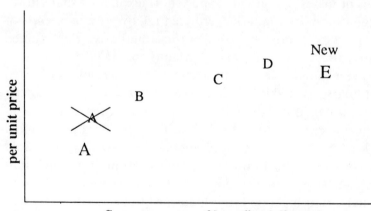

Now it's likely that A and E will gain share and that B, C, and D will lose share (although B, C, and D may misread A as a junky product that consumers will soon reject).

however. Deciphering product value often requires use of techniques like conjoint analysis that uncover the purchase trade-offs consumers make. And in industries in which there is substantial discounting of any type, or in which prices are established through a bidding process or are based on bundling several products and/or services together, even determining one's own average price per product model can be an arduous task. Nonetheless, for companies facing unexplained share losses or participating in industries in which the definition of a good deal is being altered by rapid changes in benefits delivered and prices charged, a detailed analysis of this sort is often essential to guiding an intelligent strategy. Without it, you may not be able to tell whether the market regards your product like the 1975 Cuisinart—or like the Cuisinart of a decade later.

A Final Caveat:
Customer Satisfaction Is Not Always Relevant

Some companies assume that this kind of analysis is irrelevant because they have "satisfied customers." But the business implications of customer satisfaction depend on competitive circumstances. If there are no better alternatives, even a "dissatisfied" customer may still be a repeat customer. Conversely, when there are many terrific alternatives, a "satisfied" customer may not be a very loyal customer. The reason is simple: *Good deals are always defined in relation to what the competition offers and at what price.* The immediate question, therefore, is not whether customers are satisfied, but whether they are convinced that they have found the best combination of price and benefits for their needs.

Take the custody business of banks, a service that arranges for the settlement and safekeeping of securities traded in national and international markets. In the 1980s in the United

States, these services were highly automated, very efficient, and nearly error-free. But in many non-U.S. capital markets, the necessary infrastructure was not yet in place for fast and efficient settlement of trades, even on a manual basis. As a result, banks that provided global custody services could not match their performance in the United States, no matter how committed they were to customer service.

Not surprisingly, when investors accustomed to the U.S. market needed a global custodian, they often were unhappy with the quality of service they received. Here's how one respondent to a 1988 survey by the magazine *Global Investor* explained the situation:

> "We have had nothing but problems with our global custodian. While at best our current custodian is inadequate in almost everything a global custodian should do, we have found them particularly appalling in the area of settlement, accounting and record keeping, and customer relations."

Although not satisfied, such customers may nevertheless stay with their current vendors because significantly better alternatives simply do not exist—yet. (If you're still not convinced, think about the dry cleaner you use. Unless you're very lucky, you may be a dissatisfied but repeat customer simply because you can't find another cleaner that is convenient with any better record of cleaning clothes without breaking buttons and mangling lapels.)

The reverse situation also occurs: satisfied customers who are not very loyal because of the range of good alternatives that exist, as is often the case for restaurants, hotels, and retail stores. When a slightly better deal becomes available, these happy customers may be on their way down the street.

The point, of course, is not that customer satisfaction is unimportant, but that the focus must be on what customers want *relative to what they can get* and what they have to pay for it. In short, there's no substitute for understanding the customer's definition of a good deal. And in the end that means considering the price/benefit profiles of a wide range of competitors.

BANK ROLLS MAKE THE WORLD GO AROUND

Costs are the other part of providing a good deal profitably, as indicated in the "bank roll test." Does that mean having to be "the low-cost producer"? The question as stated, though frequently debated, is nonsensical. Products, such as Porsches, that have a medium to high value don't have to match the cost basis of their lower-value competitors (although it's quite advantageous when this happens). What they do need to strive toward is the lowest costs *relative to their product-value position.*

Looking at the costs/benefits profile of your products versus your competitors' is therefore essential to figuring out how to make a buck. (For those who still like graphs, now let the y-axis show total product cost and keep the x-axis showing total product value, as shown in Figure 6-2.) Why is having the lowest costs relative to product value so important? Because whoever has such cost advantages can use them in one of two strategic ways: the company can either make more profit than its competitors and plow that profit back into better products or a lower cost position, or it can use its higher margins to drop prices today to protect or gain market share.

Take Two Aspirin and Call Me In the Morning

Understanding competitors' costs is a powerful way to anticipate likely reactions to strategic moves. Bristol-Myers found this in 1975, when the company decided to introduce its own acetaminophen product, Datril, to compete with Johnson & Johnson's Tylenol.

Bristol-Myers' strategy was simple. The company positioned its product as the same pain reliever with the same

Figure 6-2 An example of a cost/delivered benefits analysis

Following the price/delivered benefits positions shown in Figure 6-1, one can see why understanding relative cost positions is so important:

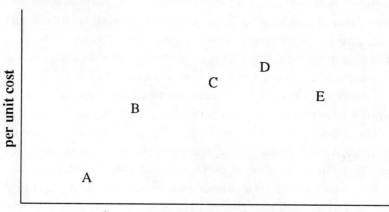

Some measure of benefits delivered

In this example, Competitors A and E are advantaged because they have the lowest costs relative to their respective positions on the x-axis; they can therefore keep their prices high, as in Figure 6-1, and have a larger bank roll that they can then reinvest in the business, or they can drop price to retain the new share they have gained at the expense of competitors B, C, and D. If B, C, or D drop price to try to regain the share they have lost, they are likely to get stuck on the wrong end of the ensuing price war.

safety as Tylenol but less expensive: $1.85 for 100 325-milligram Datril tablets versus $2.85 for the same amount of Tylenol. But Tylenol's brand-management team—James Burke (subsequently chairman of J&J), Wayne Nelson, and Jack Zeigler—decided to meet Datril's price, issuing credit memoranda for current in-store stocks so that all prices would be at $1.85. They also moved aggressively to expand the product's distribution by adding grocery stores to the list of outlets where Tylenol could be purchased.

Johnson & Johnson's cost position provided the company with the pricing flexibility to respond swiftly to the Bristol-Myers threat; according to advertising executives Al Reis and Jack Trout, even though the total product cost also included marketing and distribution costs and the like, the direct cost of the acetaminophen itself was in the range of five cents per hundred tablets. The result was little success for Datril, while Tylenol increased its share of the painkiller market.

There's No Such Thing as Cost Strategies Versus Value Strategies

Was Johnson & Johnson pursuing a "value-driven" strategy or a "cost-driven" strategy? Many companies try to categorize strategies as based *either* on the benefits delivered to consumers (often referred to as "differentiation"), *or* on their cost position. But, as used in practice, the first tends to lead to actions based on the premise that customers are interested only in the benefits they receive, so that both price and therefore internal costs are relatively unimportant. The second tends to lead to the reverse; actions based on the premise that customers are only interested in price, so the company need only focus on its own costs and not worry about other benefits that consumers could want.

Some companies, for example, explain their strategies as being "value-driven" or as providing better "quality" to the discerning customer. What they often mean by this is that they do not think they have to pay attention to their costs because they believe that *their* customers are "not price-sensitive"; in other words, they believe that if their costs go up, they can just raise their prices and their customers will still buy their products. And they may be correct, until a competitor figures out how to offer those same customers a better deal by providing equivalent benefits at a lower price or greater benefits at the same price—as manufacturers of cars, cameras, and countless other products have discovered.

Similarly, other companies describe their strategies as "cost-driven." In these strategies, costs are cut, sometimes without careful consideration of the benefits associated with these costs. But *which particular costs* are cut affects the consumers' valuation of the benefits being delivered and therefore can change their perception of whether they will get a good deal if they purchase this product.

In short, there's no such thing as "value-driven" strategies or "cost-driven" strategies. There are only strategies that lead to attractive cost positions relative to the delivered benefits, and strategies that don't.

IN SEARCH OF PROFIT

Companies must control their costs in order to deliver a good deal to the customers while making a profit for themselves; that's obvious. But doing so doesn't always mean cutting costs, and certainly doesn't mean cutting costs across the board in a "cheese slicer" approach that shaves an equal amount from every department. Instead the answer is to cut the costs that don't add enough value from the customer's point of view, and to assess whether there are new costs that could deliver disproportionately high value. For example, should a car-repair shop get rid of the loaner cars it allows customers to use when their cars are in the shop? Direct Tire, a Watertown, Massachusetts, enterprise has eight such cars, which cost it $28,800 per year. But Direct Tire's owner calculates that adding the loaners also adds about $780,000 in annual revenues to his shop at attractive gross margins. Since the costs deliver disproportionately high customer value that in turn accounts for a very large revenue stream, it would be foolish to cut them.

Finding the Source of the Disadvantage

Competitors that can offer the same set of benefits for lower costs mean trouble. Responding to this threat therefore requires understanding the sources of the cost disadvantage and determining whether and how it can be overcome. Frequently the analysis will show the culprit to be either a cost or a competitor that is usually overlooked.

Take the case of the blue capacitor. As creativity guru Roger von Oech tells the story, a company caught in a cost crunch discovered that one part of their problem was a single-sourced component, a capacitor. Why was that capacitor chosen and would it be possible to use another? A trip through five levels of management finally led to the designer and his answer to the question: "I chose it because it's blue, and it looks good on the circuit board." That choice effectively added hidden nonproductive costs to the manufacture of the product.

Indirect costs and overheads are another set of costs that are easily overlooked. Consider the findings of consultant Ira Magaziner's analysis of GE's microwave oven business in 1983, showing that the typical microwave oven that cost GE $218 to produce cost Korean manufacturer Samsung only $155. A portion of this difference was in direct costs; the cost of assembly labor per oven was $8 for GE and 63 cents for Samsung.

But the biggest difference was in indirect costs—from overhead labor, to materials handling, to line and central management—amounting in total to $44 for GE versus *87 cents* for the Koreans. Magaziner's analysis was cause for alarm. Even taking into account the premiums that GE could achieve due to its brand name, channel access, and service network, the magnitude of its cost disadvantage could force the company into a series of trade-offs between margins and market share: price lower to maintain market share, or price higher to maintain unit margins. The numbers were ultimately convincing. In 1985, GE announced that it would cease all domestic microwave oven production, using Samsung as its supplier instead.

Why are overheads often a hidden source of nonproductive costs? One reason is that the relationship between indirect costs incurred by the company and benefits delivered to the consumer can get lost. Without a clear link, these costs can grow, fulfilling Parkinson's Law, which states: "Work expands so as to fill the time available for its completion." Parkinson's inspiration for his law illustrates how this happens:

> "I was serving in a joint headquarters [during World War II] . . . and the headquarters was headed by an air vice marshal, who was assisted or possibly impeded, by a colonel in the army, who was impeded, or possibly assisted, by a wing commander in the air force, and then all three of them were assisted (but definitely assisted) by me. . . .

> "But the day then came when the air vice marshal went on leave. Shortly afterwards, as it happens, the colonel fell sick. The wing commander was attending a course, and I found I was the group. And I also found that, while the work lessened as each of my superiors had disappeared, by the time it came to me, there was nothing to do at all. There never had been anything to do. We'd been making work for each other."

Companies are also often surprised by their cost disadvantages after it is too late or almost too late to take constructive action. This is especially likely to happen when entire companies or technologies are left out of a company's analysis because they are too difficult or too different to understand. A manufacturer of specialized textiles fell into this trap when it carefully analyzed the cost structure of all the domestic producers but made no mention of the effect of foreign competitors, despite the fact that imports held about a third of the market. When a manager from another department questioned the exclusion of what were clearly important competitors, he was greeted by looks of surprise and then told that the "non-U.S. producers fell outside the analysis."

A large communications company that used satellites as part of its transmission system made a similar mistake when it modeled its future demand in great detail (calculated out to multiple decimal places for the next 20 years) without reference to a competing technology, fiber optics. When a new manager in the satellite group asked about the effect of fiber optics, he was at first politely ignored. When he pressed his question, he was finally told that including fiber optics was too complicated, so the technology had been left out. And that meant the demand calculations were also wrong, because for major communications trunks, transmission via fiber optics can cost much less than transmission via satellite.

One can only wonder why anyone in either company had gone to the effort to create such precisely incorrect models. In both cases, even educated guesses or good back-of-the-envelope analyses would have been far more valuable (and less costly) and could have led to earlier corrective actions.

Finding a Way Out

Understanding the relationship between costs to the company and value to the consumer means that sometimes the way out of a disadvantageous cost position is to add costs. For example, if you were losing money, would you be willing to do the following:

- As the head of an airline, invest an additional $45 million in capital projects and $12 million in annual operating expenses so you could conduct a punctuality campaign, improve one traffic hub, offer service courses for 12,000 employees, and restore the olives to customers' martinis? Jan Carlzon did as part of his turnaround of SAS, even though the company was headed toward a $20 million loss. The result was an $80 million improvement in the bottom line for the year.

- As the head of a forklift company, invest in a $100 million capital improvement program so you could pass along a substantial portion of the savings to your customers in the form of lower prices? Leo McKernan did as part of his turnaround of Clark Equipment in the same year that the company lost over $60 million. The result three years later was a steady increase in earnings—and a stock price that had tripled.

- As the head of a chain of nine oil-change shops, increase weekday staffing from three to five people and weekend staffing from five to seven people so you could cut waiting time for potential customers even though the average car already is in and out in 15 minutes? Larry Bartlett did as part of his turnaround of Lube 'n Go, even though his profit margins had declined to something under 1 percent. The first year's result led to profit margins in the 6 percent range, as more customers began to use Lube 'n Go—and began to buy more services on each trip.

All three of these strategies worked because, in addition to cutting nonproductive costs, these companies were willing

170

to add costs that would lead in the future to either lower average costs to the company or higher average benefits for which the consumer was willing to pay a premium. Costs per se are not the problem; it's costs that don't produce enough value to the consumer that hurt margins.

• • •

In the mid-1970s, Schlitz Brewing Company, holder of the number two share position in the U.S. beer market, set about to cut its costs. The savings came from a new process for shortening the brewing process and using corn syrup to replace some of the more expensive barley malt. The reported result was beer with visible flakes of yeast, less of a head, a taste that many considered inferior to the original Schlitz, and returns by the truckload with handwritten notes from outraged wholesalers proclaiming their views of the new beer. By 1985, the company held just one percent of the market.

Costs, prices, and delivered benefits are all part of one dynamic equation. Trying to alter one without understanding the impact on the other two is strategic folly.

THE ECONOMIC EQUATION IS MORE
LIKELY TO BE ALIGNED WHEN MANAGERS:

- Avoid blanket decision rules that suggest consumers will evaluate low-priced products as junk or view high-priced products as too expensive

- Have the analysis that allows them to understand their product's relative *price*/delivered benefit position

- Have the analysis that allows them to understand their product's relative *cost*/delivered benefit position

- Undertake product redesigns or cost restructurings based on an understanding of which delivered benefits are associated with which particular costs

CHAPTER SEVEN

--- ✦ ✦ ✦ ---

We Understand What
Our People Want

THE EMPLOYER PERSPECTIVE ON THE
INTERNAL CONTRACT, ACCORDING TO GROUCHO MARX,
FROM THE MOVIE *COCONUTS:*

Bellboys: "We want our money. . . .
We want to get paid."

Mr. Hammer, the manager (Groucho): "Oh—you want
MY money? Is that fair? Do I want your money?"

THE ASSUMPTION:

We know what our employees want.

THE REALITY:

Most companies misread the internal market.

THE RESULT:

Both the employees and the company lose.

SOME COMMON SIGNS WHEN
THE INTERNAL CONTRACT IS OUT OF KILTER

- When you're honest with yourself, you have to admit that the company is losing some of its best people.

- In their exit interviews, most people tell the same story and that story also happens to be seen as the "acceptable" way to leave.

- It's broadly assumed that the only thing employees are looking for is more money for the same amount of work (or less work for the same amount of money).

- There is little internal "market research," and most of what is done is not done on an anonymous basis.

- Employees of one of your competitors seem a lot more enthusiastic about working with their employer to win in the marketplace.

Imagine yourself confronted with the following situation. A major faction of your blue-collar work force has gone on strike. Although you can probably replace the picketing employees, the situation is complicated by the fact that another group of workers, all high-level white-collar professionals, is also considering walking off their jobs. If this happens, it's more than likely that you will lose a pivotal piece of your empire, which you have spent years building.

The good news is that it should be relatively easy to placate the white-collar workers, for a number of reasons: First, they are well aware of the difficulties they will have finding jobs at other companies, and even if they do find work, they understand that regardless of their experience, rules in this particular industry will require them to start over again at the bottom of the ladder. Second, in the past they have not been supportive of their blue-collar colleagues in the other union. Third, they are politically conservative as a group and are not generally predisposed to strikes. Finally, and most important, their demands can be satisfied without breaking the corporate bank or harming the company's overall strategy.

The obvious approach to the problem? Bend over backward to keep the white-collar workers on the job. In the real story— Eastern Airlines, 1989—just about the opposite happened.

Here are the facts of the matter. With the Eastern machinists on strike, CEO Frank Lorenzo faced a simple reality: keeping the Eastern empire intact depended almost solely on whether the Eastern pilots would cross the machinists' picket lines and keep flying. So in a last-minute move, Lorenzo sent all the pilots a video, describing a new pilots' union agreement that, he claimed, "would protect the careers of Eastern's pilots." But Lorenzo left a few details out of his talk—such as the loopholes in the agreement that diminished the amount of protection afforded by the agreement, not to mention the $64 million per year in benefit cuts that were also included in the fine print. Worst of all was the tone of the video itself. Said one pilot, "It was like he was saying: 'Come . . . children. Enough of this foolishness.' "

The history preceding the video also played an important role in the pilots' decision. In his zeal to cut costs, Lorenzo had treated the pilots in ways that they believed were unfair and unnecessary. One such cut was the decision to strip the pilots of their prerogative to give passengers free drinks when flights were delayed for lengthy periods. When a pilot complained, a company spokesman dismissed the concern with the comment, "He's just upset because he can't give away somebody else's whiskey." Though measures like these resulted in small savings, they also exacted a major cost to the morale of the pilots, to whom they symbolized the loss of both status and autonomy within the company.

In the end, convinced that restoring their self-respect was more important than protecting their financial self-interest, the Eastern pilots voted to strike. On the picket line, one pilot, a 23-year veteran of the company, explained his ballot this way: "Soon there'll be nothing, but we at least made a stand."

His assessment was exactly correct, for both the pilots and for Frank Lorenzo. For an alternative approach to this situation, maybe Lorenzo should have considered these words of nineteenth-century novelist George Eliot:

"Fancy what a game of chess would be if all the chessmen had passions and intellects, more or less small and cunning; if you were not only uncertain about your adversary's men, but a little uncertain about your own; if your Knight could shuffle himself on to a new square on the sly; if your Bishop, in disgust at your Castling, could wheedle your Pawns out of their places; and if your Pawns, hating you because they are Pawns, could make away from their appointed posts that you might get checkmate on a sudden. You might be the longest-headed of deductive reasoners, and yet you might be beaten by your own Pawns. You might be especially likely to be beaten, if you depended on your mathematical imagination, and regarded your passionate pieces with contempt."

WELCOME TO THE INTERNAL MARKET

For all the lip service paid to it, few organizations spend as much time trying to figure out their employees as they do trying to understand their customers. But the basics of strategy apply as much to the internal market as they do to the external market. In both cases, the company is in the role of the seller. And in both, the goal is to provide what the buyer sees as a "good deal" in a way that allows the company to be profitable. The primary difference is that when the employees are the customer, they "pay" in effort rather than cash—and they can adjust what they pay at any time according to their perception of the quality of the deal that the company offers them.

Because the currency of their internal market is effort, employees "buy" into the corporate program by staying on and giving everything they can. The corollary is that every time a company doesn't provide a good enough deal within its own four walls, employees "pay" a little less—do a little less, offer a little less, care a little less. If they consider the deal to be bad enough, they will either cut back and do only the minimum required to keep their jobs, or they will leave, either to find other jobs or to go on strike, as Eastern's pilots did.

Many companies don't like to think of their employees as customers; it seems to confuse the lines of power within the organization. But providing a good deal profitably between any buyer and any seller is always a matter of negotiating an agreement that satisfies the needs and wants of both parties. And the balance of power in the negotiation always depends on

179

the alternatives each party has. The conclusion is inescapable: If you need what these buyers have to offer—which is their wholehearted commitment to the enterprise—you'd better figure out what they consider to be a good deal and what you have to do to offer it to them profitably.

The Theories

Figuring out what a good deal means to the internal market is one of those subjects that tends to evoke reactions based on deeply held assumptions about "human nature" instead of observations of reality. The argument most typically revolves around three views of what people really want: more money, more leisure, or more autonomy.

Those who argue that it all comes down to money might point to the recent experience of Levi Strauss in Hungary. Setting up its operations in half of a state-owned plant, Texcoop, the company doubled the workers' wages (on the condition that they not accept any outside work), and then broke all records for productivity and quality, even exceeding the company's own profit projections by a factor of two. Life on the other side of the plant, still working under Texcoop rules and incentives, remained the same as it had been before Levi Strauss came to town, with two-thirds of the equipment sitting idle and absenteeism running at close to 25 percent.

Those who argue the second point of view, that what most employees really want is to spend as little time working as possible, might side with Frederick Taylor, the turn-of-the-century industrial engineer. Taylor put his model of human nature this way: "Hardly a competent workman can be found who does not devote a considerable amount of time to studying just how slowly he can work and still convince his employer that he is going at a good pace." Managers who agree with Taylor might point to the recent experience at GM's Flint,

Michigan, plant where, after management threw out the time clocks, workers suddenly found ways to produce their quotas of parts before the lunch whistle blew.

And finally there are those who argue that a company's employees want to do a good job, if only management would "empower" them to do so. These people might point to the dramatic turnaround at SAS and suggest that success of companies like this is due primarily to the intrinsic rewards that workers receive when they are given greater autonomy in the execution of their jobs.

The Data

Which of these three points of view is the best approximation of reality? Though managers often operate on the basis of one of these mental models of what employees want, simple observation would suggest that most people are motivated by all three objectives, but in differing proportions. The corollary observation is that the employees of one company might, as a group, have a different profile relative to these three objectives than those of another company, or that the profile might vary from country to country.

An interesting source of data comes from Daniel Yankelovich, the famous pollster, who has been studying American workers and what they seek from the workplace for most of the second half of the twentieth century. His research indicates that the old post-World War II implicit contract between U.S workers and their employers—hard work, loyalty, and steadfastness in return for a steady paycheck—has been superseded. Without question, fair compensation for effort expended is still required. But in addition, working people in the U.S. today are looking for, *and expecting*, greater nonfinancial returns than ever before.

Given a list of 46 job characteristics, in 1982 a representative sample of the U.S. working population, including both blue-collar and white-collar employees, rated the following ten as "very important":

Preferred Job Characteristics
(percent of sample rating these characteristics as "very important")

Working with people who treat me with respect	88%
Interesting work	87%
Recognition for good work	84%
Chance to develop skills, abilities, and creativity	83%
Working for people who listen if you have an idea about how to do things better	83%
Having a chance to think for myself rather than just carry out instructions	83%
Seeing the end results of my efforts	82%
Working for efficient managers	79%
A job that is not too easy	78%
Feeling well-informed about what is going on	78%

In contrast, 64 percent of the sample rated both the "opportunity to make as much money as I am capable of making" and "good retirement benefits" as very important.

These results do not suggest that money is unimportant. The survey did not include a statement along the lines of "fair pay for effort expended," which might have achieved a higher ranking than the statement used, "opportunity to make as much money as I am capable of making." And it did not use a conjoint design, which would have permitted a more precise understanding of the relative importance of each of these characteristics. Still, the overall message is valid: For Americans as a group, work is not purely a financial exchange between a profit-maximizing individual and a profit-maximizing enterprise. Working people in the U.S. expect their jobs to enhance their self-worth as well as their net worth.

When It Takes More Than Money

Sometimes the discrepancy between what employees really want and what their managers think they want is extreme. Consider the case of a company we'll call Spaulding Technologies, which had become concerned (and appropriately so) about a continuing exodus of key people. In their exit interviews, most of the departing employees said they were leaving because of the considerably higher compensation they could receive at other firms. Spaulding's president had one question he wanted answered: Exactly how much more would Spaulding have to pay to keep its best people?

Subsequent interviews of seven key people who had jumped ship revealed an unexpected finding, however. Of the seven defectors, *only one* had actually left primarily because of compensation. For the other six, the primary reason was that the nonfinancial part of the equation had become so unsatisfactory that they could no longer justify the compensation discount from what they could earn elsewhere. The one who had made the decision for financial reasons was unequivocally happy with his new job; the others still felt that they had made the right decision but would have preferred staying at Spaulding if the problems could have been fixed—three to the point that tears welled up in their eyes as they talked about their old company.

In fact, both the ex-employees and the current employees agreed that Spaulding already provided many elements of what they saw as a good deal. They believed in the company's mission of contributing to society and felt real pride in being associated with a company that stood for those kinds of values. They liked the feeling of being part of the Spaulding "family" and were challenged by their jobs. And they placed a high value on an environment that was intense but not all-consuming—a person could work hard at Spaulding and still have a real life outside the firm.

But even the people who stayed were aware of and unhappy with the downside of the Spaulding equation. Most of them felt that there was no real link between the quality of their work and either pay increases or timing of promotions. Another problem was that Spaulding was organized as a pyramid, with a broad base and a very steep and narrow hierarchy. Little room at the top limited the opportunity for increased compensation. More important, however, it meant few opportunities for promotions, external recognition, or participation in the internal management of the company.

The companies that raided Spaulding for its best people offered a different kind of deal. The missions of these companies were less attractive to a Spaulding person because they focused exclusively on making money rather than contributing to society; there was little feeling of family; and the work environment was intense and all-consuming. But the structures were broad enough at the top to offer enormous potential for external recognition and internal say in key decisions. And these companies offered compensation packages 50 percent or more higher than those the Spaulding people were currently earning.

For the type of people that Spaulding liked to attract, therefore, bringing compensation up to parity with the other recruiters, while the obvious solution, was not the best solution. In fact, in both interviews and written surveys of current employees and the new interviews of those who had left, Spaulding people voiced the strong opinion that staying at Spaulding was worth a substantial discount—*if* the problems involving external recognition, internal participation in decision making, and the link between financial rewards and performance could be fixed.

With a fuller understanding of the situation, management at Spaulding set about enlarging the top of the pyramid and completely restructuring the compensation system, while simultaneously working to preserve the other aspects of the work environment its employees greatly valued. One result was higher compensation, although still not nearly so high as that of the raiding recruiters. But the more significant result was a revised internal contract that not only met the needs of the employees, but did so in ways that also made Spaulding a stronger organization. The investment paid off: turnover was dramatically reduced and employee enthusiasm skyrocketed. Not coincidentally, so did Spaulding's success in the marketplace.

REDEFINING A GOOD DEAL

In some ways, buying a truck or a breakfast cereal is not very different from figuring out where to seek employment and how much commitment to make to a job; both kinds of decisions require making trade-offs in which certain shortcomings are accepted in order to gain other desired characteristics. There are, of course, some key differences. When customers are unhappy, they can usually switch. When employees are unhappy, they are more likely to switch off.

Even so, the basic parallel holds. Few jobs are an ideal match. Therefore, employees, like customers, develop an implicit set of "score-board" values that they use as they trade off what they see as the benefits of their jobs against what they see as the drawbacks. So the question becomes, do you know enough about what your people want that you could design a good deal for them that also works to the advantage of your company?

Give-Me's and Let-Me's

A mutually advantageous agreement like the one developed at Spaulding requires consideration of both the financial and non-financial benefits employees seek. But while financial benefits are usually easy to analyze, nonfinancial benefits tend to be elusive. Complicating the matter is the fact that there are two types of nonfinancial benefits, and they differ fundamentally in the ways they motivate people.

The first type of nonfinancial benefit is the "give-me's," which make work life more agreeable and the job more pleasant: a comfortable cafeteria with good food, for example, or a work location with ample covered parking. Sometimes employees seek give-me's because they reduce the amount of work they must do, as occurred at GM's Flint, Michigan, plant, for example. At Spaulding, two of the give-me's that increased employee satisfaction were congenial co-workers and a reasonable life-style. A third give-me that employees sought, but did not have, was nicer working space—almost all the professionals worked in cramped and poorly ventilated bull pens with little individual work space and virtually no privacy.

The second type of nonfinancial benefit is the "let-me's." These fill a different kind of need, because they make the substance of the job itself and the future of the company an intrinsic part of the employee's motivation. The let-me's at Spaulding included interesting work, challenging standards, and the goals implied by the company's mission. The deficits in this area, from the employees' perspective, included the lack of participation in management decisions and the lack of differentiation between those who did a good job and those who did not.

Whether a characteristic is a give-me or a let-me, and how important it is to the internal contract, is an individual perception that varies from person to person and from group to group. Figuring out what characteristics a particular group of employees is seeking and whether they perceive each of these attributes as a give-me or a let-me is therefore very important. It is the least risky way to match employee wants with employment characteristics. More important, since the let-me's have far greater motivational power than the give-me's, this understanding is an invaluable asset in creating mutual advantage for a company and its employees.

Yankelovich and his colleague John Immerwahr tested this proposition by asking the respondents in their sample to evaluate each of a set of employment characteristics in terms of its motivational power. Their results can be displayed to show which characteristics add to people's desire to do a good job and which simply make work more pleasant without adding to the motivation to do better. Two-thirds of the respondents, for example, said that "a good chance for advancement" would increase their commitment to doing a good job, while just under a quarter said that "a convenient work location" would have the same effect on them. The complete results are summarized in Table 7-1.

Welcome Back the Work Ethic

A work force with a large number of people who desire the let-me's is a work force with a high work ethic. And despite those who bemoan the passing of the work ethic in the U.S., Yankelovich's data suggest that the American willingness to work hard is alive and well, with just over half the U.S. work force meeting this criterion. According to Yankelovich, the problem is not so much the workers as it is the jobs, many of which are not structured to take advantage of the workers' let-me's—exactly the situation that Spaulding faced.

Table 7-1: Perception of Job Attributes as "Let-Me's" and "Give-Me's"
(percent of U.S. respondents with this perception)

	Adds to Motivation to Do a Good Job	Makes Job More Pleasant Only
Let-Me Characteristics		
Good chance for advancement	**67%**	22%
Job enables me to develop abilities	**61%**	27%
Pay tied to performance	**59%**	31%
Recognition for good work	**58%**	34%
Job requires creativity	**55%**	31%
Job allows me to think for myself	**54%**	33%
Interesting work	**54%**	35%
Challenging job	**53%**	30%
A great deal of responsibility	**50%**	28%

Of course, not all employees are willing to increase their commitment to doing a good job. Yankelovich's data also indicate that about one-fifth of the working population in the United States say that they are either unwilling or unable to give more to their jobs than they are already giving, no matter

Table 7-1 (continued)

	Adds to Motivation to Do a Good Job	*Makes Job More Pleasant Only*
Give-Me Characteristics		
Fair treatment in work load	44%	**45%**
Being informed about what goes on around here	37%	**49%**
Flexible working hours	33%	**49%**
Flexible work pace	32%	**49%**
Get along well with supervisor	31%	**52%**
Working with people I like	30%	**52%**
A job without too much rush and stress	28%	**61%**
Workplace free from dirt and pollution	24%	**56%**
Convenient location	24%	**56%**

what else is done. But think about the flip side of that statistic: Almost four-fifths of the U.S. work force would invest *more* in their jobs if their managements would invest more in helping them to do so.

Interestingly, Yankelovich's data do not suggest that a strong work ethic is a universal situation. With his colleagues, Yankelovich conducted similar studies in Japan, Israel, Sweden, the United Kingdom, and (then-)West Germany. For German and Japanese workers, for example, the story is quite different than in the U.S. The data from the German study, headed by Bernhard Strumpel, suggest that only one-quarter of the total West German work force has a strong work ethic, and that German workers in general "appear to be somewhat 'fed up' with the work ethic; they want to take a more relaxed attitude toward the world of work." The Japanese data, on the other hand, show a work ethic profile that is similar to that in the U.S. with one major twist: Just over half of young Japanese workers (under the age of 29) say they are primarily committed to themselves rather than to their employers. (By comparison, only about one-fifth of Japanese workers over the age of 55 answered that question the same way.)

Regardless of country, however, let-me's represent a real bonus for both employers and employees. Any company lucky enough to have a profile like Spaulding's should jump at the chance to provide its employees with what they want, because fulfilling more of the let-me's works to the advantage of both the company and the people it employs.

Tough Managers, Soft Benefits

Some managers have a difficult time grappling with give-me's and let-me's—the stuff of the internal contract—because they see these issues as "fuzzy" or "touchy-feely." This perception often stems from a sense of managerial machismo and a belief that only the "tough" survive. Here's how one retired executive explains the perceived need for "toughness":

> "Some time ago *Fortune Magazine* came out with their list of tough managers. By their criteria, although not mentioned in their article, Pug Williams, who took over after I retired, could be classified as a 'tough manager.'
>
> "Williams had a golden opportunity. A new broom sweeps clean and, let's face it, there was fat in that company that could have been trimmed and he would still have had a great organization. But Williams's definition of 'tough' drove some of our best people right out of the company.
>
> "Case in point. Jack DiMaggio was the regional sales manager of the Southeast—our most productive region. He was a great salesman and a very effective manager of people. Williams recognized DiMaggio's abilities but tried to make him a hatchetman—firing other people. DiMaggio couldn't take it and quit. This happened all over the country. Not only were good men fired, but many of those who were not fired became totally demoralized and quit.
>
> "Williams took control of a company whose people were deeply motivated, destroyed their pride in the company, and ended up losing over $100 million in sales.
>
> "So when they talk about tough managers, I say, tough against whom? Tough against their own people. So I say to you, these people are not tough managers. They're stupid patsies!
>
> "A tough manager is one who is *tough on the competition.* That's being tough!"

Keeping important people like DiMaggio happy does not mean pampering them or allowing them to avoid the tough decisions that they must make. But it does mean that the internal contract has to take into account an understanding of employee needs and wants; it must serve the interests of the individual as well as the organization.

Noise In the System

Two barriers often stand in the way of finding this balance between the needs of individuals and the organizations in which they work: cultural differences between groups of managers and their subordinates, and the idiosyncratic style of any individual manager. The problem of cultural differences is likely to be a growing issue, as the world economy becomes more intermingled. Yankelovich's data, for example, which show differences in the expectations of workers in various countries, suggest that miscommunication in the negotiation of the internal good deal is a particular risk when workers and managers come from different cultures.

Japanese/American relationships can be particularly tricky. Japanese managers typically scold more and praise less than Americans are accustomed to, and this difference in cultural style can result in unintended messages between Japanese and American employees working in the same company. Or as Atsushi Kageyama, president of an American subsidiary of Panasonic, explains: "Japanese rarely praise others because they are uncomfortable when others praise them. Praise is confused with flattery, and flattery is a cause for mistrust."

There is also the matter of subtle symbols that mean different things in different countries. Consider this recent experience of American workers in Mazda's Flat Rock, Michigan, plant, where everyone had accepted the Mazda uniform of khaki shirts and blue trousers. And then came the issue of the baseball caps, explained as a voluntary accessory to the uniform. Some people wore the caps and some did not, which upset the Japanese managers in the plant. Even though the caps were voluntary, according to Joseph and Suzy Fucini, who studied the Mazda facility, the Japanese "regarded not wearing caps as a sign of disrespect toward the company. When the Japanese pressed the issue, the Americans countered that cap wearing was voluntary. True, the Japanese acknowledged, but if you really cared about the company you should *want* to wear your caps. The Americans, who could accept being told what they *had* to do by an employer, took offense at being told what they should "want" to do. . . . *Mandatory-voluntary* was the term they began to use to describe the company's directives." In short, rules that may have made perfect sense in a Japanese context were difficult to understand in an American one.

Even without a cultural overlay, individual managers can dramatically change how good the deal appears to the company's employees. This apparently happened at Value Line, Inc., when the company began to lose some of its most important senior people, including Peter Lowenstein, the general counsel, and Mark Tavel, the head of investment management. Though the principals aren't talking, *The Wall Street Journal* suggested that the problem had to do, at least in part, with the managerial style of Jean Bernard Buttner, daughter of the founder, who took over the firm after her father's death at the end of 1987. Imagine the day that Buttner entered Lowenstein's office, conducted a "room inspection," declared the office to be too messy, and ordered Lowenstein to have it cleaned up by that evening. Lowenstein reportedly was irate at the intervention. While this is not a big event in the cosmic scheme of things, it is the kind of incident that can lead employees to say, "Life's too short," and then either walk out or cut back on their effort.

Or consider the new CEO of an information-services group who was transferred into a division in which profitability was heavily dependent on the productivity of a group of software developers. This CEO had not managed software developers before, but one thing was immediately clear to him: they didn't dress like businesspeople, and he intended to remedy the situation. Shortly thereafter a dress code was announced.

Keeping software developers happy is something of an art. It is not unusual to find flexible hours, pinball machines, and beds as part of the rarefied environment in which these people work. And although there may be a brilliant software developer somewhere who wears a blue suit, white shirt, and red tie, as a group programmers consider casual dress to be a prerogative and a symbol of their transcendence of business norms.

The dress code therefore went into effect, but at a steep price. The programmers' casual attire had not affected the other employees, who accepted the need for software developers to be treated differently than the rest of the work force, and it had not affected customers' perceptions, because customers never saw them. In the end, while it made the CEO feel better, it severely damaged the morale and enthusiasm of a group on which he needed to rely.

In some ways, of course, office decor and business attire may not seem to be matters of great consequence, especially if the offices or people are not going to be seen by customers. But as in the case of Eastern, it's the little things that come to take on great symbolic value for the people in the organization; they are metaphors for how the employees *think* they are perceived and appreciated. Matters like these therefore become significant factors in the internal good deal, either as incentives or disincentives for continued commitment. For this reason, their importance can hardly be overestimated.

THE COST FACTOR

Obviously, a company can afford to provide a good deal to its internal customers only within certain cost constraints. Providing a good deal to employees in a way that is profitable for the organization often requires a juggling act in which some costs are cut while others are added.

Eliminating the Costs That Sap Morale

Quality experts frequently make the claim that good quality costs less than poor quality. The same argument applies to providing a good deal profitably to the internal market (which, of course, is part of total quality). The reason is that hidden costs sap motivation, especially that of the most committed employees.

Mindless policies that cause employees to shake their heads in disbelief as they carry on their work are a particularly dangerous source of hidden costs because they pack a double whammy: they add absolutely no value and pose a huge cost to morale. One common villain (but by no means the only one) is paperwork: stacks of reports to review and stacks of reports to fill out. Under Reginald Jones, the managers of one of GE's businesses got seven *daily* reports, *each of which* created a pile of paper 12 feet high. At many other companies, managers routinely spend large amounts of time filling out and reviewing complex forms, the objectives of which could be achieved with far less paperwork. For all, the sheer volume of paper and figures tends to obscure the handful of data and issues that are most important to running the business.

Perhaps the ultimate example of mindless activity was revealed in the experiment conducted by psychologist Ellen Langer and two colleagues, who sent out an interdepartmental memo in a university setting. The memo had one of two messages. One read, "Please return this immediately to Room 247"; the other, "This memo is to be returned to Room 247." That was the *complete* text of both memos. The results were startling. Despite the complete absurdity of the instructions (and the fact that there was no Room 247 in the building), most of the memos were returned. As Langer pondered, why didn't the recipients ask themselves, "If whoever sent the memo wanted it, why did she or he send it?" and then throw the thing out?

Langer argues that organizations are full of routines and procedures that result in activity that detracts from the organization's productivity. How do you root out these kinds of activities? One way is to ask people inside the company—they generally already know where many of the nonproductive and counterproductive requirements are.

Adding the Costs That Build Commitment

Frequently, costs have to be added in order to provide a deal that is good enough to keep employees buying. Not surprisingly, one of the most frequent excuses for not renegotiating the terms and conditions of the internal contract is that it would be too expensive to do so. At Atlantic Enterprises, the parent company of Spaulding Technologies, for example, some thought that the new plan for opening the top of the organization represented an unjustifiable cost. Yet Atlantic was the biggest winner of the new approach taken by Spaulding; with its turnover dramatically reduced and enthusiasm high, the subsidiary grew dramatically in terms of both financial performance and customer perception.

Another new cost that is often required is increased *effort* spent on evaluating and rewarding employees. Many employees in U.S. companies, for example, do not think their contributions to corporate performance are likely to be rewarded. Just 22 percent of the respondents in the Yankelovich and Immerwahr survey thought there was a close link between an individual's performance and pay in their organization. In contrast, 28 percent saw only a partial correlation, and 45 percent saw no link at all. The requirement for creating the link, therefore, is not incremental cash for payments to employees but incremental time and attention from managers to evaluate performance and communicate progress.

But sometimes direct cash payments to employees are also called for as prudent investments in increased commitment. Gain sharing, in which part of the profits or savings from employee efforts is distributed to some or all employees, is primary among these. The power of gain sharing is basic: many people are willing to make a greater commitment to doing a good job—if they can expect to share in the results.

Such payments typically arouse little attention when they are limited to high-level white collar personnel, such as the investment bankers in a Wall Street firm or the top executives of a manufacturing concern. But what about plans that touch everyone in an organization? For the past 40 years, Herman Miller, Inc., an office furniture manufacturer located in Zeeland, Michigan, has used a Scanlon plan, in which all employees in the enterprise have generated ideas for improving performance and have shared in the rewards. A part of the gains goes into each worker's paycheck, and the other part goes into the company's coffers.

Why should Herman Miller give away part of these gains? For this company as for others, the basic calculation is the same. If most of the work force has achievement needs that are not being adequately fulfilled, and if these needs can be channeled into activities that improve the organization's ability to serve its customers profitably, why not take advantage of an untapped asset? As with any other kind of return, sometimes you have to spend money to make money.

• • •

Money may make the world go round, but many people seek more than money from their jobs. Or as one entrepreneur explains his motivation: "My personal view is that corporations are the means that men and women of vision use to extend their reach."

While other people may have other motivations, one generalization remains valid: managing without understanding the good deal calculus used by the internal market of employees makes no more sense than delivering goods and services without understanding the good deal calculus used by the external market of customers.

MUTUAL ADVANTAGE IS MORE LIKELY
WHEN MANAGERS:

- Think about giving the internal market "a good deal at a profit"

- Try to understand the "let-me's" employees seek, as well as the "pay-me's" and "give-me's"

- Routinely do internal market research, with at least a substantial portion done on an anonymous basis

- Periodically undertake open-ended research to make sure the internal research is asking the right questions

- Use as much creativity for designing a "good deal" for the internal market as they would for the external market

CHAPTER 8

◆ ◆ ◆

Our People Know What to Do

*The executive art is nine-tenths
inducing those who have authority to
use it in taking pertinent action.*

—CHESTER BARNARD

THE ASSUMPTION:

Everyone knows what to do
and how to do it.

THE REALITY:

Each person in an organization makes on the
order of a hundred decisions a day (but not
necessarily the right ones).

THE RESULT:

The company's people can become a competitive
disadvantage.

SOME COMMON SIGNS WHEN THE
DAILY HUNDRED AREN'T ON TRACK

- A competitor consistently seems to have some sort of invisible edge when it executes its strategy.

- Somehow it seems that only the bare minimum ever gets done.

- The commonly held belief among senior managers is that once they have made the big decisions, all the decisions that materially affect the organization have already been made.

- The prevailing belief is that what needs to be done "should be obvious" to everyone in the organization.

- Other people in the organization often seem to use poor judgment when they have to make decisions.

- What people do to get ahead is significantly different from what they think they would do if this were *their* business.

- The people who get rewarded are not the people who do what the organization *says* it wants people to do.

For years, the Ritz-Carlton was the only place to stay in Boston if you could afford the rates and were willing to lighten your wallet. The hotel itself, a magnificent old building overlooking the Public Garden and providing a sweeping view of the city, has a location that's hard to beat. Add its elegant furnishings, historical prestige, and renown for outstanding service, and it's not surprising that in 1989 the Ritz was one of only a handful of hotels in the United States to have earned the American Automobile Association's coveted five-diamond rating.

What was surprising, however, was AAA's 1989 award of the five-diamond rating to a newcomer two blocks away, the Boston Four Seasons hotel. That same year the local press published the following overall comparison:

A report card

	Four Seasons	*The Ritz*
Overall	A	B

PUTTING ON THE RITZ

How did the formerly undisputed queen of the Boston hotel market end up with a mediocre B, while an upstart garnered an A? According to the reporter responsible for the "report card," it was the smallest of the daily decisions made by the personnel of the two hotels that made the difference. On the expanded version of his report card, in fact, he gave the Ritz a nod on the big-ticket items: its ambiance of romance, its chef, and its legendary bar. But where the Four Seasons pulled ahead was on the small-ticket items, the myriad of nearly invisible decisions that a hotel's employees make every day as they do their jobs. Here are a few examples of why the reporter gave the higher overall rating to the Four Seasons:

- The doorman at the Four Seasons was smooth and efficient, while at the Ritz, the doorman "failed to open the door of the car [on the passenger side], became confused about the luggage, neglected to close the car door, and then failed to assist with the revolving door."

- The bellhop at the Four Seasons was patient and professional, but at the Ritz the bellhop seemed rushed: "while he offered to get ice, he also spoke so rapidly and moved about so swiftly and departed so quickly that he was disconcerting."

- The room at the Four Seasons was ready for its visitors, but at the Ritz "service was again a problem, for the bedsheets were torn along a seam, and the floor had not been vacuumed well."

- The restaurant maitre d' at the Four Seasons was courteous and accommodating. At the Ritz, by contrast, the maitre d' seemed miffed and was curt, never even acknowledging a request for a table by the windows when he seated the reporter and his guest in the middle of the dining room.

- Room service was "impeccable" at the Four Seasons, but "disappointing" at the Ritz where, having asked that three newspapers be delivered to his room, the reporter received one paper in full, the second in part, and the third not at all.

In short, the Four Seasons became a competitor to be reckoned with—not just because of its strategy, but because each person on its staff knew what to do at multiple decision points during the day and then *chose* to take these actions.

WHEN DISCRETION IS THE BETTER
PART OF VICTORY

Whether a company operates a hotel chain or manufactures chain-link fences, the issue is the same: it's the little on-the-job decisions people make every moment of the day that can make the difference on the competitive report card.

Despite their importance, however, these decisions are easy to underestimate and difficult to manage. Small in comparison to the strategic decisions taken by senior managers, they are far more numerous. Some do not even seem like decisions at all because they are characterized by the *lack* of action—an effort not taken, an idea not pursued. Yet whether the outcome is to act or to do nothing, each time a person is confronted with a choice, a decision is made, and that decision either supports or goes against the goals of the organization.

At the Ritz, for example, the doorman and the bellhop could have extended themselves a bit further, the housekeeping service could have paid closer attention to the ripped sheet and the dirt on the carpet, the maitre d' could have forced himself at least to appear to be sorry that he couldn't comply with a patron's request. These decisions to hold back—to fail to act, to go by the book when a better solution exists, or to withhold a suggestion or an idea—happen all the time. A line worker may decide to allow a potentially defective part to slip through the assembly line; a salesperson may not provide that little extra encouragement or piece of information to close a sale; a marketing person may not suggest a product revision that could increase revenues. All of these are examples of unused discretion, the ability of each person to make judgments and then act on them in ways that further the goals of the organization as a whole.

Why isn't the power of discretion better harnessed in organizations like the Ritz? Part of the problem is that while the number of decisions involved is huge and their collective impact is enormous, they can rarely be controlled directly. The answer therefore is to create an environment that makes it easier for each person to do the right thing.

A Hundred Decisions a Day

Just how many decisions does the average person make during the course of a workday? A reasonable guess is about a hundred. Of course, the actual number varies from job to job and from person to person, and even from day to day for the same person. But there is considerable evidence that a hundred decisions a day per person is in the right ballpark—or, if anything, is an underestimate.

Researcher Henry Mintzberg, for example, once "shadowed" the chief executive officers of five large organizations for a week each, tracking their activities from the moment they came to work on Monday morning to the time they turned out the lights on Friday. By Mintzberg's tally, these CEOs divided their average day into 15 work sessions with other people, either in meetings or by telephone, and seven desk-work sessions devoted to the review of 36 pieces of correspondence and other written materials. Each of these 15 meetings and 36 documents in turn required decisions, either to wait and do nothing for the moment or to take one of a range of possible actions.

The situation faced by top executives of smaller companies does not appear to be any easier. In a similar kind of observational study in three organizations, Irving Choron found that the presidents of these smaller companies divided their average days into 77 discrete activities, each of which again required decisions.

It would be tempting to assume that this variety of activity, and the decisions each activity requires, simply reflects the realities of life at the top. But for middle managers as well, the data show the same pattern of many daily activities. By monitoring the activities of 56 foremen, yet another researcher observed a range of 237 to 1,043 activities a day, with an average of 583. "Every forty-eight seconds of the day," this researcher noted, "the foreman was doing something different."

But are all these actions really the result of employees using discretion in the daily conduct of their jobs? Elliott Jaques would argue that they are. Jaques has conducted in-depth observations in 15 countries in organizations as diverse as the United States Army, the Glacier Metal Company in the U.K., the Church of England, and CRA, an Australian mining company. Based on these observations, he developed the concept of the "time-span of discretion," which he defines as the "maximum time during which the manager must rely upon the discretion of his subordinate and the subordinate works on his own." His conclusion is that discretion and choice are part of every job, although the nature of this discretion varies by the level within the company.

To take a practical example, the largest choices facing an airline gate agent might result in upgrading a ticket, holding a plane at the gate, or refusing to board a drunken passenger. The decisions facing the CEO of the same airline, however, may revolve around the proper hub arrangement for flight routings, the aircraft to be used for the fleet of the future, or the company's negotiating posture with labor. In contrast to the gate agent's decisions, the time span from the initial consideration of a CEO's decisions to the moment of their final implementation can be on the order of years rather than minutes, with far greater uncertainty about their effects. Despite the difference in the nature of the choices, however, both the gate agent and the CEO are decision makers, each facing many decisions every day. Or in Jaques's words, *"Exercising judgment and making decisions is what you pay people (everyone) for."*

In addition to the preceding evidence, logic also suggests that everyone in an organization makes multiple decisions every day. After all, work life is a constant stream of choice points about what action to take or whether to act at all: whether to speak in a meeting, whether to smile at a customer or patron, whether to stop a production line, whether to let work stand that has been done incorrectly, or, as in the case of the Ritz, whether to change torn sheets, vacuum the rugs, smile, or just slow down enough to make sure that the guests have a chance to respond to the information being provided. From this perspective, a hundred decisions a day is, if anything, an underestimate of reality.

The Multiplier Effect

A hundred bad or good decisions a day multiplied by all the people within an organization pack a cumulative wallop. But their importance exceeds their collective numbers, for even the smallest of these decisions can have lasting consequences, especially when they deviate from the organization's espoused strategy. The handful of people responsible for the B rating at the Ritz, for example, demonstrate the multiplier effect. Even if none of them intentionally sabotaged the hotel's image, they certainly picked the wrong times to act in ways that didn't support the establishment's vision of perfection. Very probably, though, these incidents were part of a larger pattern: in 1990, AAA downgraded the Ritz to four diamonds, while keeping the Four Seasons at five.

For some senior executives, there is no doubt about the potential impact of decisions that take only moments to make and implement. SAS's Jan Carlzon is one of these. By his figuring, SAS's ability to move from a money-losing to a money-making proposition depended on each of the 136,986 decisions made daily by the company's front-line employees, based on the following calculation: SAS annually serves 10 million customers who, on average, spend 15 seconds with each of the five SAS employees with whom they come into contact. The result, in Carlzon's words, is that "SAS is 'created' 50 million times a year, 15 seconds at a time. These 50 million 'moments of truth' . . . ultimately decide whether SAS will succeed or fail as a company."

Moments of truth like these work to the advantage of the company only when people know how to use the discretion inherent in their jobs. Yet their real impact on any organization can be easy to overlook because the costs of wrong decisions often are virtually nonverifiable, even when the repercussions are lasting. Consider the case of a woman, now the executive vice president of a midsize company, who has never shopped again at a major prestigious retail chain since the day, 20 years ago, when she was ignored by three salespeople even though she was one of only two customers in the department. The other customer, an older woman with the air of inherited money, was making a small purchase but was evidently a regular at the store and known by name. None of the three made any effort to attend to the second customer until the first one had left, which took about 20 minutes. Here's the perspective of this former customer on what transpired:

> "I didn't mind the waiting, but I was really angry about how I was treated. While I was waiting, none of the sales staff made eye contact with me or acknowledged my presence in any way. Maybe the other two were busy with another task—it didn't look that way but you never know. But the third fellow just looked through me, like I wasn't there. He didn't say, 'I'll be with you in a while' or 'This will take a few minutes more. Why don't you look around?' Not even a nod to show that he knew I was there. And when he finally did wait on me, he never apologized for the delay. *He made me feel like a nobody. I made my purchase, but I have never set foot in any of their stores again and I never will.*"

With her furs and perfectly coiffed hair, the older woman may have been the very image of the kind of customer this store likes to attract. But the younger woman represented, by her own calculation, perhaps 60 years of future revenues to the famous chain of stores. The cost to the company, however, was invisible—she never complained, she just never came back. Hearing this account, two colleagues began to nod and told a similar story about the same company. "I only shop there for those few things I can't find at other stores," one explained. "Otherwise I prefer to shop elsewhere."

An unusual story? Probably not. In a survey conducted for *The Wall Street Journal* with a sample of 2,064 people, fully 60 percent said that they too boycott stores because they are unhappy with the way that they have been treated. Among professionals and those earning more than $50,000 per year, the percentage was even higher—about 75 percent. In short, a single small decision by one employee can cast a long shadow.

The disproportionate effect of a single decision may be more apparent in the front line, high-contact nature of the service industry. The decisions made in the back room or on the factory floor can be just as important, however, ranging from corners being cut in the design and manufacture of a product to slow order processing or lax enforcement of material handling policies.

Bad decisions like these are usually the consequence of people not knowing what they should do or not being convinced that it is worth their while to make the effort. And sometimes, of course, they are the product of outright sabotage as when, several decades ago, disgruntled workers at GM and Ford reportedly put an occasional loose bolt into Cadillacs and Lincoln Continentals to create rattles or, more recently, when someone at Cracker Jack substituted a miniature sex manual for the regular prize in the box. But in either case, the point remains: Taken as a whole, the hundred decisions a day of each person in the organization can have consequences that exceed even those of the most brilliantly thought-out strategy. The heart of the matter is therefore to determine whether the people in your company know how to use the discretion inherent in their jobs, and whether you want to *control* that discretion or *encourage* it.

TO CONTROL OR TO ENCOURAGE; THAT IS THE QUESTION

When some managers realize the collective power of other people's daily decisions, their first instinct is often to clamp down in order to eliminate discretion from their subordinates' jobs. Often this approach is fueled by the widely held theory that, in the words of one textbook, "Responsibility and authority must be coequal if people are to be held accountable for results in a given area of activity." In other words, the theory is that managers need to have enough authority to control the actions of the other people through whom they work.

You Can Write a Script to Order . . .

But the question is one of feasibility rather than theory: is it possible to script a job so completely that people don't have to make decisions? For example, how many times have you walked into a fast-food place and been greeted by someone with a clearly phony smile, who growls something like, "Mayihelpyouplease?" The facial expression and words may meet the specs perfectly, but you know the difference between this tape recording and people who smile with feeling or ask, "May I help you?" as though they really mean it.

Theory aside, in the United States, at least, the evidence is that most people in the work force see discretion as an

213

already-existing characteristic of their jobs. In the Yankelovich and Immerwahr study cited in Chapter 7, for example, almost two-thirds of the 845 respondents said that in their jobs they had "a great deal" of discretion over quality, and almost half claimed "a great deal" of freedom in deciding how to do their work and the effort they put into their jobs.

And in all likelihood, the proportion of the work force with high-discretion jobs will increase in the future. One reason is the growth in white-collar and service-sector jobs, both of which typically involve high levels of discretion. Another source of the increase will be growth in jobs in which technological change plays a major role. Rather than reducing discretion, advances in technology actually tend to increase the scope of decision making. In fact, Yankelovich and Immerwahr found that almost three-quarters of those who had experienced such changes over the past five years said they found their jobs more interesting as a result, and more than half said that such changes had resulted in greater independence in their jobs.

But if supervisors can't directly control every decision of their subordinates, then a boss's authority can never be coequal with his or her responsibility. The solution to the dilemma is therefore to think in terms of influence rather than control. This approach flies in the face of the common metaphor that managers should be like orchestra conductors, able to command every aspect of every worker's job with just a wave of the baton. But even orchestra conductors don't have that kind of control. Consider this comment from one longtime player in a world-renowned symphony orchestra:

"A great conductor can get you to do what he needs with the minimum gesture but the maximum respect. He lets you know what he expects from you and then he uses the baton to acknowledge that he knows you can do it. He balances the systems within the orchestra and sets the broad picture and then lets you use your discretion for the rest. The more standard conductor, on the other hand, micromanages to the point that individuals can't play or are so angry they don't want to."

In short, although each person's daily hundred decisions are beyond direct control, they are not beyond influence. The most compelling reason for managers to pay attention to these decisions is the executional advantage that can be created when the right decisions are made consistently across the organization, as the Four Seasons and SAS both demonstrate. And, conversely, the risk of the wrong hundred decisions being made is the creation of an organization that is its own worst enemy, incapable of coordinated action.

. . . But You Can't Make It Think

Companies that want these daily decisions to be a competitive advantage need to create informed discretion among their employees. The obvious place to start in this task is with the organization's official words, the overt messages it sends in its public pronouncements and publications. Many techniques and styles can be used to make these messages clear and compelling, ranging from internal advertising campaigns to factory-floor discussions—the only requirements being respect for the intelligence of the audience and constancy of the message. Or as former British Prime Minister Margaret Thatcher once advised her party's members of Parliament: "Keep your nerve. Keep what you believe in and go on explaining what you are doing and why."

But the official words are only a small part of the equation. Much more important are the ongoing managerial decisions within an organization: Few signals are more powerful than who gets the largest compensation increases, the fastest or most prestigious promotions, or the most glamorous assignments—and who is slowed down, left behind, or terminated. And behind these larger messages are many smaller ones sent by what managers do every day. In total, these managerial *actions*, large and small, define the internal game of the organization; they describe what to do to get ahead and suggest the loopholes from accountability that savvy players can use in their efforts to speed the process. When the official words don't match the actual decisions, one thing is for certain: subordinates will learn to speak the script—and play the game; in other words, they will exercise their discretion in ways most likely to be rewarded and will avoid those that are likely to garner no rewards or, worse, to be punished.

Trying to script employees so that they have no degrees of freedom is therefore an illusion: it is almost impossible to achieve and often leads to demoralized the staff and inhibited creativity. The alternative of creating an environment in which employees are encouraged to develop and use their judgment, on the other hand, requires managers to face a subtle but difficult task: figuring out what the *real* internal game is (corporate rhetoric notwithstanding), determining how well it matches with the requirements of the organization's strategy, and then changing it (and themselves) to eliminate the mismatches.

AN UNLIKELY SUCCESS STORY

Across town from the Ritz and the Four Seasons sits an unlikely example of an organization that keeps most of the hundred decisions a day of its employees aligned with its strategy: Boston's Beth Israel Hospital. Why are data about a hospital useful to for-profit corporations? Because in many ways, hospitals like the BI provide a worst-case situation. Not only are they under intense pressure to cut costs, but they also have very little control over pricing, limited flexibility regarding the services they offer, and very difficult customers—patients and their families who are facing illness, pain, and the possibility of death. The BI's dilemma is more extreme still, since it will not turn away customers who don't pay. The result is a true managerial nightmare, featuring tremendous problems with few degrees of freedom for solving them.

Yet in the face of such problems, Beth Israel's experience shows how the determination to expand the judgment exercised by each person within an organization can make the difference between average and outstanding performance. Twenty-five years ago, the BI was a community hospital with a weak university affiliation and a mixed reputation at best; today it is one of Harvard Medical School's major teaching hospitals and is nationally regarded as a top-flight institution. Here's a little of the supporting evidence for that claim:

- *The Best Hospitals in America* listed the BI as one of the 64 best of the nation's 6,500 short-stay hospitals.

- *Healthcare Forum Journal* counted the BI as one of America's ten most successful hospitals, and the only one in Boston included on the list.

- *Business Week* rated the BI as one of America's five best-run hospitals in the country, and the only one in Boston on the list

- *The Service Edge: 101 Companies that Profit from Customer Care* cited it as one of the U.S.'s best service organizations in any industry, and one of only three hospitals (and again the only one in Boston) to make the list.

The introduction to the *Service Edge* write-up summarizes one of the mysteries of the BI's reputation: "When you ask Boston doctors to name the best hospital in town, chances are they'll say Massachusetts General. . . . But a funny thing happens when you rephrase the question and ask them where

217

they would go for treatment if they or someone in their family had to be hospitalized. Then the answer you're likely to get is Beth Israel Hospital."

More important than these reviews, however, are the results of an internal look at the hospital, conducted by Harvard researcher and Harman Fellow Elizabeth Glaser. Glaser's research agenda was straightforward: Do the people at the BI *really* live up to their collective reputation? And if so, how does each person know what he or she is supposed to do?

The BI's official words paint a picture of a hospital committed to marrying the forefront of medical science with the highest degree of human care and respect for patients and their families, or as one BI physician calls it, "medicine with grace." This is not an unusual message; what hospital would say anything else? Finding the answer to Glaser's research questions therefore required direct observation of what actually happens on a daily basis. So, in addition to the usual evaluation of patient comments, review of patient focus group transcripts, and in-depth interviews with 48 people throughout the organization, Glaser adopted the methodology Henry Mintzberg used in his observations of CEOs—following people around as they did their usual tasks. But instead of "shadowing" one executive for a week, Glaser spent about two months of actual time shadowing 23 people, each over the course of at least one shift. Among these 23 were nurses and housekeepers, surgical residents and food tray servers, chiefs of service and phlebotomists.

Using this methodology, Glaser's research showed a high correlation between the BI's corporate statements and the decisions of its 4,600 employees. Two reasons for this similarity of words and actions stood out in particular: (1) the pervasive use of personal examples and persistent coaching to show people how to fulfill the BI mission, and (2) the creative use of systems and structures to reinforce the desired behaviors. In other words, in most ways the internal game matched both the hospital's strategy and its official statements. (Interestingly, "training" was not a factor. As Laura Avakian, vice president of human resources, explained, the BI has to turn down the frequent requests it receives to share what outsiders assume to be its remarkable training programs. The reason is not that the programs are proprietary, but rather that the training programs being requested simply do not exist.)

The BI data are useful because it's rare to have public access to the inner workings of an organization, particularly one that has been as successful as the BI has been in making the internal game an asset. These data do not provide a prescription for creating informed discretion, though, since there probably are as many ways of doing this as there are organizations. Instead they suggest two key questions managers should ask themselves as they move to line up the internal game with the kind of informed discretion they seek to create in their own organizations:

- What do each of us *do* each day that demonstrates what we really reward?

- How do we help stack the deck to make it easier for people to do the right things?

The answers to these questions determine whether the internal game serves the goals of the organization or takes on a life of its own.

AN APPLE A DAY:
FIGURING OUT WHAT IS REALLY REWARDED

The BI's success begins with the leadership of the hospital's president, Dr. Mitchell T. Rabkin. For a quarter of a century, Rabkin has worked to articulate the hospital's mission and make it a reality. Demonstrations of commitment to this mission start at the top and range from the largest managerial actions to the smallest; one gets accustomed, when walking with BI people, to waiting while they occasionally stoop down to pick up stray pieces of trash. Explained a chief of service (and one of the most senior doctors in the hospital), "Mitch picks up paper from the floor, so I do too."

(As an aside, this is why Rabkin picks up the trash: Shortly after his appointment as president of the hospital, he was visited by a trustee who invited him for a little stroll of the facilities. Stopping at one patient floor, the trustee suggested to Rabkin that they pick up every other piece of trash they happened to spy. He then took Rabkin to a second patient floor, where they wandered around and chatted, but didn't pick up any trash. Shortly thereafter, they visited the two floors again. On the first one, most of the remaining trash was now gone; the second was as messy as it had been before. The moral of the story according to the trustee: "Never think you're so fancy that you can't pick up the trash. If you don't do it, why should anybody else ?")

But what Rabkin does is only part of the story. While corporate leadership is important, in any organization it's the immediate supervisors that usually have the greatest effect in transmitting the real rules of the game. They hold the keys to promotions, and how they manage their people on a day-to-day basis tells their subordinates what they think "doing a good job" means.

The Messages Are the Medium

Managers send all different types of signals to their subordinates, and the signals can be explicit or implicit, positive or negative. At the BI, Glaser found the management signals to be explicit, positive, and unceasing. BI people learn what doing a good job means primarily by the continuing stream of sug-

220

gestions and praise they receive. Or as Joyce Clifford, vice president of nursing and nurse-in-chief explains, "we have a socialization process, not an orientation process." Here are a few examples of how the environment of coaching and feedback works at the BI:

- A nutrition supervisor gives her employees the following pep talk every day before they hit the floors: "All right, now remember what you are supposed to do out there. Knock on the door, smile, say hello, and put down the tray." One of the food servers later explains that the supervisor always gives a pep talk; it wasn't just for show because an observer was there.

- A housekeeping supervisor describes his job: "I talk to them about the importance of saying hello when they go in the room. I think that it's important. They don't need to speak English just to be nice, polite and say hello." A manager of the hospital's laundry services shares a similar philosophy: "I spend a lot of time trying to get the people in the laundry to understand what is going on and understand that what they do is patient care too."

- A nurse manager explains why she puts so much emphasis on coaching: "I believe there is a relationship between happy employees and satisfied patients. I learned a lot about this behavior from my mother. I have also learned a lot about this from my boss."

- And then there was this comment from the chief of surgery, emphatically confirmed by the residents in his department: "At the Beth Israel, being concerned with the patient isn't regarded as being 'soft.' Other hospitals would say that isn't sufficiently macho, but you don't do well here if you are abrupt with patients."

221

The frequency and constancy of the message make their mark. One physician, looking back over his career at the hospital, describes the effect this way: "I don't know what it is about the place. But when people come to the BI, if they are not of the BI way, the institution changes them. I have spent a lot of time thinking about this and I don't have the answer, but it changes them."

Somebody Else's Job?

People at the BI were adamant about the importance of coaching and feedback in their own development and viewed these practices as the cornerstone of their own philosophies of managing others. But is this the norm in most U.S. organizations?

Not according to the findings of Harvard Business School professor John Kotter, who surveyed approximately nine hundred senior executives from just over a hundred firms. Kotter was interested in the ability of these firms to hire, develop, motivate, and retain the kind of star performers who could step into top leadership positions. In the area of the development of talent, where coaching and feedback are most important, the results were especially disappointing. Asked to rate a variety of practices used within their companies on a four-point scale—more than adequate, adequate, somewhat adequate, or inadequate—most executives used the last two categories to describe their companies.

Here are three highlights from Kotter's results:

- *Only 7 percent* of the executives rated "the way managers are rewarded for developing subordinates" in their organizations as adequate or better.

- *Only 21 percent* rated "the mentoring, role modeling, and coaching provided" in their organizations as adequate or better.

222

- *Only 25 percent* rated "the way feedback is given to subordinates regarding developmental progress" in their organizations as adequate or better.

As one of the respondents to this survey commented, "When you talk to our middle-level managers about this, they essentially say—'Give me a break. My job is to make my quarterly plan or budget. It is someone else's job to worry about that other stuff.' "

BI's Mitch Rabkin would disagree: "We try to make all our staff in the hospital aware that they are role models, that you are what you do, just as you are what you eat. This attitude has to go everywhere, it's not just teaching them the *content* of medicine, it's teaching them *how* to be doctors, and it's the same with our managers. Subordinates always observe those above them anyway, so we try to use the opportunity consciously."

STACKING THE DECK:
MAKING IT EASIER TO DO THE RIGHT THINGS

Sometimes the games inside companies, although satisfying to the internal combatants, impede people from doing what is needed to meet the organization's goals. Preventing this situation requires finding organizational mechanisms that support doing the right thing. At the BI, among the primary mechanisms are the recruitment process, the design of front-line jobs, and an innovative ideas program. Other organizations do it differently; regardless of the techniques chosen, however, the goal should be the same: to stack the deck to make it easier for people to use informed discretion.

The Right Stuff

Obviously, hiring the right people is critical to the success of any organization, but the way various organizations go about the hiring process differs considerably. Federal Express, for example, has developed detailed profiles of the kind of person who succeeds in each of its various positions, from customer agent to courier. Other companies use structured interview guides and tests of all sorts—written and verbal, psychological, and skills-based.

Beth Israel Hospital takes yet another tack, using an intensive process of relatively unstructured interviews. A middle manager comments: "I couldn't believe how seriously they took the interviewing process. When I came here, I interviewed with thirteen people, from the medical director to the unit coordinator [a clerical position]." The point of all these interviews is the same as that of the more formal methods used in other companies: to find people who are a natural fit with the BI approach. A nurse manager describes her criteria this way:

"I look for values in the people I hire. I try and get a sense of the person. The kinds of questions that I ask include those which get at values through situational questions. If the person answers the question with a remark about some technical aspect of care, then they are a very different person than one who will tell you a personal story about some aspect of care. I don't think any of my staff asks this question in the same way, but I suspect that as they talk to people, they try to figure out the same things."

At the heart of the BI method is an overriding concern with fit. Not everyone responds well to a particular organizational mindset; what is a mutually reinforcing and satisfying situation for one person can be a painful environment for another.

"Fit" in fact is a double-edged sword, because by definition people who don't share the dominant mindset are likely to be unhappy in environments in which fit has been emphasized. Look at Nordstrom's department stores, seventh heaven for all dedicated shoppers. Many "Nordies" are enthusiastic about their jobs and find the pressures of sales quotas and motivational techniques stimulating. They are the ones that fit the Nordstrom's mindset and mission. Some, however, do not. As one saleswoman in the latter camp confided, "It's a very intimidating environment. They preach that as long as you're giving service, they'll take care of you. But that's not true. All they really care about is how much you sell." Not surprisingly, Nordstrom's expands only into markets in which they think they will be able to employ "their" kind of people, and even then transfer large numbers of Nordstrom veterans into a new store to ensure that the customer-oriented environment gets off to a good start.

Structure Follows Function

Companies today often talk about "inverting the pyramid" or "flattening the pyramid," but the first and most important (and often ignored) step is understanding what each group of employees could do to contribute to the company's ability to provide "a good deal" to its customers. At SAS, for example, Carlzon realized that what travelers thought about the airline depended heavily on their interactions with gate agents, cabin attendants, and baggage handlers. By defining these people as the company's front line and restructuring the company around them, Carlzon created a tighter linkage between goals and roles. As Carlzon points out, while going after the full-fare business traveler was neither a fresh nor a particularly brilliant idea, its execution was.

Almost fifteen years before Carlzon's actions at SAS, the BI came to a similar realization. Although patients may select a hospital on the basis of a physician, a great deal of the patient's satisfaction and medical outcome depends on the quality of nursing. When Rabkin joined the BI, nursing was

225

one of the most serious problems—continuity of care with each patient was spotty at best and the care often did not combine human warmth with technical excellence. With the recruitment of Joyce Clifford as nurse-in-chief, however, the BI developed and pursued an idea that revolutionized the hospital: assigning each patient to a primary nurse who coordinates and is accountable for all of the patient's nursing care while the patient is in the hospital, and replacing the role of Head Nurse with Nurse Managers who, in effect, are the general managers of their units.

Redefining nursing in this way has yielded many important benefits. Collaboration between nurses and physicians has increased, and the nurses are better able to deliver personalized care to patients and their families. In turn, patient care has improved, as has the satisfaction of the nurses. As a result, in a market plagued by acute nursing shortages, the BI still attracts the kind of nurses that it seeks. And despite its success, Clifford and her colleagues are now further refining the nursing role to match new changes and opportunities in health care delivery.

Many companies can't do what SAS and the BI have done, however, because they don't truly understand how to use the discretion inherent in each job to contribute to achieving corporate goals or aren't willing to make the changes required to support such discretion. The evidence is easily seen in the new "empowerment" programs at many other airlines and the new "primary nursing" programs at many other hospitals that somehow haven't yet made the expected impact.

Inviting Everyone to Shape the Future

The BI story is still evolving. Across the country, the economics of running a hospital, especially one that is university-affiliated, are becoming more and more difficult. For many, the trade-off is simple: cut costs and reduce quality.

Like all other medical institutions, the BI is caught in the same squeeze. But knowing that it had to reduce costs and yet unwilling to forego quality, the BI set upon an unusual solution: adopting a Scanlon plan that invites everyone in the hospital to share ideas about how to increase quality and reduce costs. The plan, now the largest in the country and the first one ever in a nonprofit, splits the resulting gains 50–50 between the employees and the hospital.

In the first ten months of the program, the hospital has saved $2,000,000, about one percent of its annual operating budget. But the importance of the program goes beyond the savings it has generated. More importantly, it is yet another way to identify the obstacles that get in people's way as they try to do their jobs well, and to keep everyone contributing their thoughts and ideas about what can be done better tomorrow and how to do it.

Of course, Beth Israel is not a perfect institution, and not everything happens the right way all the time. Rapid changes in reimbursement policies at the state and federal level have forced the hospital to cut costs, leading to difficult choices about crowding and the amount of personal attention that can be devoted to patients and their families. The BI's Scanlon plan is a new approach to managing with many bugs yet to be worked out. In addition, the hospital is still experimenting with ways to identify and then eliminate nonproductive costs that make it difficult for people to do a good job. That said, the BI provides one example of how a company can turn its personnel into its strongest competitive advantage. The point, of course, is not that the BI has found "the answer." As long as the internal game supports the organization's goals, there's almost no limit to the ways of encouraging employees to use the discretion inherent in their jobs. The "answer," in fact, is unique to every organization; the only true commonality is the commitment to building on the hundred decisions that each employee makes each day.

• • •

A Federal Express driver comes to fetch a 7:30 p.m. pick up, the last of the night. But the customer she meets is muttering that if he had ten minutes more there would be five packages instead of two. Without missing a beat, the driver goes out to her truck, comes back with a pile of envelopes and address forms, and asks the customer if 45 minutes more would be sufficient time to get the other packages in order.

Why had the driver gone to this effort? This was her reasoning: "It was the right thing to do. I knew I could do my other pick ups, and then swing back. And I knew if I came back he would have more packages to send and that next time he would call Federal Express again and not go to UPS or someone else." She was correct, of course. But she was not required to do more than make the 7:30 pick up, nor was she paid a "bounty" for packages in excess of orders received, nor was there a supervisor in the truck. In fact, there was no one telling her what to do and why she should do it.

Employees' good judgment, and their will to use it in their hundred or so small decisions a day, can be a company's most important competitive advantage.

THE DAILY HUNDRED ARE MORE LIKELY TO BE A COMPETITIVE WEAPON WHEN MANAGERS:

- Recognize the power of other people's hundred decisions a day

- Review *what* really gets rewarded by reviewing *who* gets the rewards—who gets promoted, who gets the best assignments, the best offices, the biggest bonuses, or the biggest raises

- Figure out the loopholes from accountability that encourage short cuts or other actions that are different from what people would do if this were *their* business

- Find the obstacles to people concentrating on and doing a good job, and then get rid of these obstacles

- Ask what else the organization could do to make it easier for people to do the right things

- Institute formal ways to solicit, evaluate, and act on employee ideas, observations, and concerns

EPILOGUE

━━━━━━━━━━━━━━━━━ ✦ ✦ ✦ ━━━━━━━━━━━━━━━━━

Challenging Corporate Truths

"I never did give anybody hell. I just told the truth and they thought it was hell."

—Harry S Truman
33rd President of the United States
known as "Give-'em-Hell" Harry

ACKNOWLEDGMENTS

— ✦ ✦ ✦ —

It's a good friend who will read a manuscript, and a really good friend who will read a manuscript and offer criticism. Robert Bettacchi, Amar Bhide, Jeff Bradach, Carol Franco, Catherine Hapka, Robert Keefe, Rand Mulford, Jim Ramsey, Albert Shapiro, Jeremy Silverman, Nan Stone, Mary Sutherland, Beth Stern, and Marjorie Williams read multiple drafts of this book and their criticisms were invaluable. My thanks also to John Dailey, Steve Mintz, Robert Ogle, Mason Tenaglia, and the patient professionals at both John Wiley & Sons and Impressions. I will miss Howard Hosbach, whose encouragement was unending, even during his last days.

In addition, I'd like to thank Elizabeth Glaser, with whom I had the pleasure of working on the Beth Israel Hospital case study summarized in Chapter 8, and Professors Robert Eccles and Nithin Nohria, who helped us shape the research; Becky Burckmyer, a wonderful editor who tried to keep my subjects and verbs in agreement and my adjectives and adverbs from coming to blows; and Bob Smith, who encouraged me to follow Plan B.

I owe special thanks to the following three people:

- John Mahaney, my editor at John Wiley & Sons, who took a chance on this book and whom I've repaid many times in aggravation (as any good author should);

- Susan Webber, my guardian drill sergeant, for whom no flight of fancy or transgression from logic was too small to be tracked down and dug out by its roots; and

■ Steven J. Bennett, who helped me reorganize and re-write the (almost-) final draft of this book, pruning overwrought metaphors, expunging sodden prose, and generally insisting on clear thinking and clean structure;

And finally, my unending gratitude is due to Trina L. Soske of the Hillcrest Group, whose razor-sharp intellect, insistence on practical solutions, and abundant common sense never let her (or anyone she works with) strive for anything less than the best. The ideas in this book were enriched immeasurably by her fundamental contributions.

NOTES

$\blacklozenge\ \blacklozenge\ \blacklozenge$

Introduction: What Competitive Traps?

p. 3   ... the first Z rolled off the boat ...
        See David Halberstam, *The Reckoning*, Avon Books, New York, 1986, pp. 442–443.

p. 4   "We have been shocked out ... "
        Quoted in Donald F. Barnett and Louis Schorsch, *Steel: Upheaval in a Basic Industry*, Ballinger Publishing Company, Cambridge MA, 1983, p. 37.

p. 4   ... the possibility of future problems had been clear: ...
        A more detailed description is provided in Barnett and Schorsch, *Steel: Upheaval in a Basic Industry*.

p. 4   ... with shutdown costs for some mills of close to $1 billion.
        Bethlehem Steel's shutdown of its mill in Lackawanna, New York, is a good example, with shutdown costs of approximately $900 million.

p. 4   The Swimsuit Manufacturers' Association ...
        See Barbara Carton, "Swimsuits Grow Up with the Boomers," *The Boston Globe*, 30 May 1989, p. 31.

p. 5   ... Northwest's management approached Fallon McElligott ...
        See Richard Gibson, "The Autocratic Style of Northwest's CEO Complicates Defense," *The Wall Street Journal*, 30 March 1989, p. A1, A8.

p. 6   ... had one of the highest rankings of airline passenger complaints ...
        See Judith Valente, "Northwest Airlines to Alter Ads, Jets

235

and Airport Gates," *The Wall Street Journal*, 19 May 1989, p. B5.

p. 6   A bus line in Great Britain . . .

Described in Patrick Ryan, "Get Rid of the People and the System Runs Fine," *Smithsonian*, September 1977, p. 140.

p. 7   . . . Amalgamated's Special Purpose Integrated Electronic Systems Division (SPIES) . . .

Fictitious name and disguised industry and company details.

p. 8   . . . how to alter the mental "tape" . . .

Many researchers have thought about the problem of mental tapes from a variety of perspectives. As a few examples: psychologist Jerome Bruner talks about "constructed worlds" and "cognitive maps" (see Jerome Bruner, *Actual Minds, Possible Worlds*, Harvard University Press, Cambridge MA, 1986, and Jerome Bruner, *On Knowing*, Belknap Press, Cambridge MA, 1979); scientist/philosopher Thomas Kuhn, about "paradigms" (see Thomas Kuhn, *The Structure of Scientific Revolutions*, 2nd Ed., Enlarged, University of Chicago Press, Chicago IL, 1970); business theorists Chris Argyris and Donald Schon, about "organizational learning," and Henry Mintzberg, about "strategic learning" (see C. Argyris and D. A. Schon, "Organizational Learning," in D. S. Pugh, eds., *Organization Theory*, Penguin Books, New York, 1984, pp. 352–371; Henry Mintzberg, "Crafting Strategy," *Harvard Business Review*, July-August 1987, pp. 66–75); businessman Arie de Geus, about "mental models" (see Arie P. de Geus, "Planning as Learning," *Harvard Business Review*, March-April 1988, pp. 70–74).

Applying these theories to business, Argyris and Schon, Mintzberg, and de Geus all highlight the importance of organizational learning as the way to keep the mental models by which decisions are made lined up with the requirements for winning. Or as de Geus puts it, "The ability to learn faster than competitors may be the only sustainable competitive advantage."

Chapter 1: We Act on the Facts

p. 17   . . . a company whose line employees. . .

See Craig Forman, "Lloyd's of London, An Insurance Bulwark, Is a Firm Under Siege," *The Wall Street Journal*, 24 October 1989, pp. A1, A20. The Institute of London Underwriters includes such giants as Cigna Corp (U.S.), Allianz Versicherungs A.G. (Germany), and Commercial Assurance PLC (Great Britain).

It should be noted that some at Lloyd's took exception to the *Journal's* portrayal of the company. Wrote M. V. Williams, chairman of the company's Business Issues Committee: "We operate from a high-tech building that has become an international symbol of modernity ... [and] last year spent £125 million on computerization." Letters section, *The Wall Street Journal*, 6 November 1989, p. A17.

p. 18   ... Kevlar, a Du Pont product with five times ...

See Steven P. Schnaars, *Megamistakes*, The Free Press, New York, 1989, pp. 129, 135. Also Laurie Hays, "Du Pont's Difficulties in Selling Kevlar Show Hurdles of Innovation," *The Wall Street Journal*, 29 September 1987, p. A1.

p. 18   ... women planning business trips were courted ...

See Leslie Dickstein, "Don't Throw Bouquets at Me," *Frequent Flyer*, August 1990, p. 16.

p. 18   ... this may be why Swissair installed ...

See Milind Lele, *The Customer is Key*, John Wiley & Sons, New York, 1987, p. 133.

p. 19   ... can you explain the Xerox engineer ...

See Lele, *The Customer is Key*, p. 119.

p. 20   ... a company we'll call Juniper Technologies ...

Fictitious name and disguised industry and company details.

p. 22   ... the case of Xerox ...

The Xerox case used in this chapter is summarized from Douglas K. Smith and Robert C. Alexander, *Fumbling the Future*, William Morrow and Company, Inc., New York, 1988.

p. 24   ... a number of sweeping actions ....

For a fuller description of GM in the Smith years, see Maryann Keller, *Rude Awakening*, William Morrow and Company, Inc., New York, 1989.

p. 24   ... GM's market share slid while Ford's grew ...

GM's share through November 1989 was just under 35 percent, although its October and November shares on a stand-alone basis were below 32 percent. See Paul Ingrassia and Joseph B. White, "With its Market Share Sliding, GM Scrambles to Avoid a Calamity," *The Wall Street Journal*, 14

December 1989, p. A1. Its final share for the year was 34.8 percent while Ford's was 22.1 percent, though it should be noted that Ford lost market share for the first eight months in 1990. See Joseph B. White, "Sluggish Auto Sales Suggest Price Isn't Right for Customers," *The Wall Street Journal*, 5 January 1990, pp. B1, B6.

The 1980 share numbers come from *Moody's Industrial Manual*, 1985, p. 1357.

p. 24 . . . $5 billion investment in the Ford Taurus and the Mercury Sable . . .

Two good sources for the turnaround at Ford and the Taurus/Sable program are: Alton F. Doody and Ron Bingaman, *Reinventing the Wheels*, Ballinger Publishing Company, Cambridge MA, 1988; and Richard Tanner Pascale, *Managing on the Edge*, Simon & Schuster, Inc., New York, 1990.

p. 25 . . . as Caldwell described it afterward . . .

See Doody and Bingaman, *Reinventing the Wheels*, p. 35.

p. 25 . . . the reaction of Saturn's top manager . . .

See Joseph B. White, "GM's Plan for Saturn, to Beat Small Imports, Trails Original Goals," *The Wall Street Journal*, 9 July 1990, pp. A1, A4.

p. 26 Product planning at Chrysler . . .

See Melinda Grenier Guiles, "Chrysler Corp., Facing Rough Stretch Again, Struggles to Cut Costs," *The Wall Street Journal*, 29 November 1989, pp. A1, A6.

p. 27 Such habits, according to Akio Morita . . .

This is a famous Sony story, as Gary Katzenstein discovered when he joined Sony on a one-year exchange program (Gary Katzenstein, *Funny Business: An Outsider's Year in Japan*, Prentice Hall Press, New York, 1989). Morita tells this story in *Made in Japan* (Dutton, New York, 1986) and reportedly it is also included in one of Morita's sections of the Japanese version of *The Japan That Can Say No*, a book authored by Morita and Shintaro Ishihara, a member of the Diet, Japan's legislature.

p. 27 . . . a computer-based education product, called Plato . . .

For a further description and the Norris quote, see "Control Data and the Vision Thing: A High-Tech Company Discovers the Bottom Line," *Barrons*, 7 May 1990, pp. 10ff. The estimates of investment come from Norris himself, who several times publicly declared that from 1963 to 1980, the company invested over $900 million in Plato before beginning to realize a profit. For a different perspective on this investment, see James C. Worthy, *William C. Norris: Portrait of a Maverick*, Ballinger Publishing Co., Cambridge MA, 1987, p. 104.

p. 27   Inventor/managers like Henry Kloss . . .

In addition to Advent, the companies Kloss has founded or co-founded include Acoustic Research, KLH, Kloss Video Corp., and Cambridge Soundworks. For more details on what happened at Advent, see the following Harvard Business School cases: "Advent Corporation (C)," 9-674-027; "Advent Corporation (D)," 9-676-053; and Advent Corporation (E)," 9-680-102; also, Thomas Baker, "Self-inflicted wounds," *Forbes*, 31 August 1981, pp. 100ff.

At Advent, a stereo equipment and projection-television maker, it was the television product that had captured the lion's share of Kloss's time and attention. Baker suggests that the prices of the company's stereo equipment were kept lower than the market would have accepted, simply because "Kloss was too busy to notice. He was pouring Advent's cash into projection televisions, a product for which he saw a booming market just around the corner. 'I wanted to produce the all-out definitive set,' [Kloss] explains."

p. 29   . . . at a company we'll call Rhone River Products . . .

Fictitious name and disguised industry and company details.

p. 30   . . . motto of "Whatever you make" . . .

A recent example is Amana's 1989 advertisement, "Long before they were building appliances, Amana people were building quality," full-page advertisement in *The Wall Street Journal*, 21 November 1989, p. A17.

p. 30   . . . George Foerstner, Amana's founder . . .

Quoted in "Amana Microwave Ovens," Harvard Business School case 9-579-182, revised July 1984, p. 6.

p. 31   . . . there are still some things it refuses to do . . .

See Robert Johnson, "With its Spirit Shaken But Unbent, Cummins Shows Decade's Scars," *The Wall Street Journal*, 13 December 1989, pp. A1, A8.

p. 31   . . . some say by as much as 50 percent.

See Jack Falvey, "A Winning Philosophy Becomes an Albatross," *The Wall Street Journal*, 25 September 1989.

p. 31   One customer comments: "Our people cringe. . . "

See John R. Wilke, "At Digital Equipment, Slowdown Reflects Industry's Big Changes," *The Wall Street Journal,* 15 September 1989, pp. A1, A5.

p. 32   . . . as anthropologist Lionel Tiger argues . . .

See Lionel Tiger, "When 'Corporate' and 'Culture' Clash," *The Wall Street Journal,* 9 April 1990.

p. 33   . . . he immediately mothballed four new Airbuses . . .

For more details on Carlzon's decision to mothball SAS's new Airbuses, see Jan Carlzon, *Moments of Truth,* Ballinger Publishing Company, Cambridge MA, 1987, pp. 46–49.

p. 34   When Colby H. Chandler took over as chairman of Eastman Kodak . . .

See Clare Amsberry and Carol Hymowitz, "Last Chance: Kodak Chief is Trying for the Fourth Time to Trim Firm's Costs," *The Wall Street Journal,* 19 September 1989, pp. A1, A18.

p. 36   At Amtrak, for example . . .

See Daniel Machalaba, "Stern Boss of Amtrak Pushes to Wean Line Off Federal Subsidies," *The Wall Street Journal,* 5 April 1990, pp. A1, A8.

p. 37   . . . Merrill Lynch's decision to downsize for the 1990s . . .
See Kurt Eichenwald, "Changing the Culture of Spending at Merrill Lynch," *The New York Times,* 4 February 1990, p. 12ff.

p. 37   Michael Lewis, for example . . .

See Michael Lewis, *Liar's Poker,* W. W. Norton & Co., New York, 1989, p. 143.

p. 37   . . . the company's campaign for change got off to a poor start . . .

See Eichenwald, "Changing the Culture." The Regan quote, cited in the article, was part of an earlier interview with Regan published in *Fortune* in 1988.

p. 39   . . . Nissan Motor Company's five-year effort . . .

See Paul Ingrassia and Kathryn Graven, "Nissan Shakes Free of Hidebound Ways to Mount a Comeback," *The Wall Street Journal,* 1 November 1989, pp. A1, A6.

Chapter 2: We Know What The Facts Are

p. 48   . . . was the senior manager at GM . . .

The car was the Cadillac Allanté; more details may be found in Keller, *Rude Awakening,* p. 216.

p. 50   . . . in a now-classic experiment . . .

The playing-card experiment and other related experiments are cited in Jerome S. Bruner and Leo Postman, "Perception, Cognition, and Behavior," *Journal of Personality*, September 1949, pp. 14–31; also in Jerome S. Bruner and Leo Postman, "On the Perceptions of Incongruity: A Paradigm," *Journal of Personality*, 1949, pp. 206–223. One reason the playing-card experiment is so well known is that Kuhn also described it in *The Structure of Scientific Revolutions.*

p. 50   Few worried that the toy would become a threat . . .

Both the Ford report and the data on the growth in market penetration of the Volkswagen Beetle are provided in Doody and Bingaman, *Reinventing the Wheels*, p. 2–3.

p. 50   . . . a favorite joke in Detroit . . .

Described in Al Ries and Jack Trout, *Marketing Warfare*, New American Library, 1986, New York, p. 60.

p. 51   . . . the Japanese cars were totally unsuited to American . . .

The initial problems of both the earliest Toyotas and Datsuns are described in Halberstam, *The Reckoning*, pp. 425–431.

p. 51   Lee Iacocca, for example, suggests . . .

See Lee Iacocca, *Iacocca*, Bantam Books, New York, 1984, p. 184.

p. 52   . . . the young woman who reportedly said . . .

See Keller, *Rude Awakening*, p. 164.

p. 52   . . . "poor imitations" of their imported competition . . .

See Keller, *Rude Awakening*, p. 164.

p. 52   . . . "What we should do . . . "

See Halberstam, *The Reckoning*, p. 429.

p. 53   . . . Katayama persisted and continually battered Tokyo . . .

See Halberstam, *The Reckoning*, pp. 431–434.

p. 55   . . . that profits come from controlling costs . . .

See Pascale, *Managing on the Edge*, p. 64.

p. 55   . . . that no one wants slow but cheap and reliable copiers . . .

See Smith and Alexander, *Fumbling the Future*, pp. 184–186.

p. 56   . . . that customers would continue to pay top dollar for rod, bar, and wire products . . .

See Donald F. Barnett and Robert W. Crandall, *Up From the Ashes*, The Brookings Institution, Washington D.C., 1986, chapter 3; it should be noted, however, that in the 1990s, minimills are entering the higher-end flat rolled product categories as well.

p. 57   . . . as real estate developer Trammell Crow did . . .
See J. Edward Russo and Paul J. H. Schoemaker, *Decision Traps*, Doubleday/Currency, 1989, New York, p. 128.

p. 59   . . . the same preference that gave the world instant photography . . .
All the information on Edwin Land in this chapter comes from Peter C. Wensberg, *Land's Polaroid*, Houghton Mifflin, Boston, 1987. Wensberg worked for Land for twenty-four years, from 1958 to 1982, first as a writer and later as executive vice president. The story about the focusing device for the SX-70 is contained on pp. 186–199 of Wensberg's book; the story about Polavision, on pp. 224–229.

p. 60   . . . the case of Keith Dunn . . .
Dunn's story is told in Joshua Hyatt, "The Odyssey of an 'Excellent' Man, *Inc.*, February 1989, pp. 63–69.

p. 62   . . . "Thiokol management reversed its position . . . "
See *Report to the President by the U.S. Presidential Commission on the Space Shuttle Challenger Accident*, Washington D.C., 1986, p. 104.

p. 63   . . . Roger Boisjoly, one of the engineers, described . . .
Roger Boisjoly's testimony can be found in the *Report to the President*, pp. 92–93.

p. 64   An executive director of a trade association . . .
See Mardy Grothe and Peter Wylie, *Problem Bosses*, Ballantine Books, New York, 1987, p. 46.

Chapter 3: We Have All the Facts We Need

p. 73   . . . customer calls to 800 lines . . .
See Brent Bowers, "For Firms, 800 Is a Hot Number," *The Wall Street Journal*, 9 November 1989, pp. B1, B6.

p. 75   . . . for the information holder to switch rather than fight . . .
For an elegant discussion of this phenomenon and the theory behind it, see Albert O. Hirschman, *Exit, Voice, and Loyalty*, Harvard University Press, Cambridge MA, 1970.

p. 75   . . . only 2 percent of dissatisfied customers complain . . .
The Nielsen Researcher, No. 1, 1974, pp. 12–13; cited in:

C. L. Kendall and Frederick A. Russ, "Warranty and Complaint Policies: An Opportunity for Marketing Management," *Journal of Marketing*, April 1975, pp. 36–43.

p. 76   . . . another indicates that 4 percent complain . . .

Cited in Lele, *The Customer is Key*, p. 61.

p. 76   . . . conclusions physics professor Richard Feynman reached . . .

See Richard P. Feynman, "An Outsider's Inside View of the Challenger Inquiry," *Physics Today*, February 1988, pp. 26–37.

p. 78   . . . at a major Japanese company, for example, Gary Katzenstein . . .

See Gary Katzenstein, *Funny Business: An Outsider's Year in Japan*, Prentice Hall Press, New York, 1989.

p. 78   . . . the story of Joseph Butare . . .

See Doug Bailey, "Gamble on Conifer Hurt Bank of N.E.," *The Boston Globe*, 5 March 1990, pp. 1, 8.

p. 80   . . . a military nuclear production plant . . .

See Matthew L. Wald, "Retribution Seen in Atom Industry," *The New York Times*, 6 August 1989, pp. 1, 24.

p. 81   . . . a division of a large publishing company . . .

Disguised industry and company details.

p. 82   . . . the saga of Harvey Gittler . . .

See Harvey Gittler, "Well, Shut My Mouth. . . Please," *The Wall Street Journal*, 9 January 1989.

p. 85   Managers conduct treasure hunts every day . . .

For a good discussion of the pervasive use of these kinds of questions and how they distort information in an organization, see David L. Bradford and Allan R. Cohen, *Managing for Excellence*, John Wiley & Sons, New York, 1984.

p. 86   When Lewis Carroll wrote . . .

Quoted in Martin Gardner, ed., *The Annotated Alice*, New American Library, New York, 1960, p. 196.

p. 88   . . . the company that did an internal survey . . .

See Claudia H. Deutsch, "Asking Workers What They Think," *The New York Times*, 22 April 1990, Section 3, part 2, p. 29.

p. 88   . . . the chemist who was asked to help redesign a . . .

This story is told in Daniel Yankelovich, Hans Zetterberg, Burkhard Strumpel, Michael Shanks, John Immerwahr, Elisabeth Noelle-Neumann, Tamotsu Sengoku, and Ephraim Yuchtman-Yaar, *The World at Work: An International Report on*

243

Jobs, Productivity, and Human Values, Octagon Books, New York, 1985, p. 163.

p. 89   . . . a company we'll call Applegate Industrial Products . . .
Fictitious name and disguised industry and company details.

p. 91   . . . Jaguar's chairman and CEO, John Egan . . .
See Lele, *The Customer is Key*, pp. 29, 167.

Chapter 4: We Know How to Win in Our Business

p. 97   . . . just one of the many unusual tactics that some employees of MiniScribe . . .
The details of the MiniScribe story come from Andy Zipser, "Cooking the Books: How Pressure to Raise Sales Led MiniScribe to Falsify Numbers," *The Wall Street Journal,* 11 September 1989, pp. A1, A8; also Andy Zipser, "MiniScribe's Investigators Determine that 'Massive Fraud' was Perpetrated," *The Wall Street Journal,* 12 September 1989, p. A6.

p. 100   A competitor, Conner Peripherals . . .
See Andrew Kupfer, "America's Fastest-Growing Company," *Fortune,* 13 August 1990, pp. 48 ff.

p. 100   . . . ex-employees of Dun & Bradstreet's Credit Services unit . . .
See Johnnie L. Roberts, "Dun's Credit Reports, Vital Tool of Business, Can Be Off the Mark," *The Wall Street Journal,* 5 October 1989, pp. A1, A22.

p. 101   . . . a company that tried to use a "Rude Hog" contest . . .
See Ron Zemke, *The Service Edge,* New American Library, New York, 1989, p. 57.

p. 103   . . . for the 29 excellent companies still publicly traded in 1985 . . .
See Michelle Clayman, "In Search of Excellence: The Investor's Viewpoint," *Financial Analysts' Journal,* May-June 1987, pp. 54–63.

p. 104   . . . chances are, if you chose a plastic laminate countertop . . .
See Barnaby J. Feder, "Formica: When a Household Name Becomes an 'Also-Ran,' " *The New York Times,* 12 August 1990, p. F12; the case study Feder cites comes from George Stalk, Jr. and Thomas M. Hout, *Competing Against Time,* The Free Press, New York, 1990.

p. 104 ... Gillette sold it to Wilkinson, a British ...

See David A. Ricks, *Big Business Blunders*, Dow Jones-Irwin, Homewood IL, 1983, pp. 123–124.; also Steven J. Bennett and Michael Snell, *Executive Chess*, New American Library, New York, 1987, p. 123.

p. 105 ... stopping an enemy convoy of armored tanks.

Quoted in Bennett and Snell, *Executive Chess*, p. 8.

p. 105 ... as Canon showed Xerox ...

See Lele, *The Customer is Key*, p. 204.

p. 105 ... as Toyota showed GM ...

See Russo and Schoemaker, *Decision Traps*, p. 17.

p. 106 ... as United States Time Company demonstrated to Swiss watchmakers ...

See "Note on the Watch Industries in Switzerland, Japan and the United States—1950–70," Harvard Business School case 9–373–090; "Timex Corp.," Harvard Business School case 9–373–080; and Michael Porter, *Competitive Strategy*, The Free Press, New York, 1980, pp. 96–98.

p. 106 ... Pepsi decided to attack the icon ...

See Reis and Trout, *Marketing Warfare*, p. 119–122.

p. 107 John Sculley, then in charge of marketing at Pepsi p. 107 ...

See John Sculley, *Odyssey*, Harper & Row, New York, 1987, pp. 20–22.

p. 107 McIlhenny Co. invented Tabasco sauce ...

See Mark Robichaux, "Tabasco-Sauce Maker Remains Hot After 125 Years," *The Wall Street Journal*, 11 May 1990, p. B2.

p. 108 Economist Thomas Sowell, for example, tells of this initial meeting ...

See Thomas Sowell, "Turning 60, Looking Back," *The Boston Herald*, 7 July 1990, p. 15.

p. 109 ... the experience of Scandinavian Airline Systems ...

See Jan Carlzon, *Moments of Truth*, pp. 69–74.

p. 112 ... the problem for AT & T's PICTUREPHONE ...

See Schnaars, *Megamistakes*, p. 88.

p. 113 ... the problem for a whole string of GM's "import fighters" ...

See Keller, *Rude Awakening*.

p. 113 ... the problem for duPont's Corfam ...

See Schnaars, *Megamistakes*, p. 28.

p. 113 ... from the *Saturday Evening Post* to ...
See "Saturday Evening Post (Revised)," Harvard Business School case 9–373–009.

p. 115 ... what Irving Janis calls "groupthink" ...
See Irving L. Janis, "Groupthink," in Andrew D. Szilangyi and Marc J. Wallace, Jr., eds., *Readings in Organizational Behavior and Performance*, Goodyear Publishing Co., Santa Monica CA, 1980, p. 105.

p. 115 ... 1989 survey of 611 executives at Fortune 500 companies.
This summary of a Forum Corp. study was reported in *The Wall Street Journal*. See "CEOs Are Out of Touch With Subordinates," *The Wall Street Journal*, 31 August 1989, p. B1.

p. 116 ... $11,000 doll house.
This story is courtesy of Peter Harris.

Chapter 5: Of Course We Know What Our Product Is

p. 124 ... the philosophy of George Washington Plunkitt ...
Quoted in James MacGregor Burns, *Leadership*, Harper Torchbooks, New York, 1978, pp. 311–312.

p. 125 As U.S. consumer interest in the ovens grew ...
For additional market share data, see *HFD*, 11 May 1985, and "Note on the Microwave Oven Industry," Harvard Business School School case 9–579–185.

p. 126 ... did not believe the expected returns would justify ...
For more details, see Ira C. Magaziner and Mark Patinkin, "Fast Heat: How Korea Won the Microwave War," *The Harvard Business Review*, January-February 1989, pp. 83–92.

p. 126 ... Western Union refused the opportunity ...
See Bruce Nash and Allan Zullo, *The Mis-Fortune 500*, Pocket Books, New York, 1988, p. 18.

p. 127 ... the president of Remington Arms turned down ...
See Nash and Zullo, *The Mis-Fortune 500*, p. 18.

p. 127 ... Harry M. Warner, head of Warner Brothers ...
Quoted in William L. Shanklin, *Six Timeless Marketing Blunders*, Lexington Books, Lexington MA, 1989, p. 75.

p. 127 ... top management at Zenith ...
Zenith's Walkman-like product reportedly was matchbook size, owl-like in shape, had earphones, and was worn around

the neck, with the necklace part of the product doubling as the radio's antenna. See Robert L. Rose, "Zenith's Return to Roots is Risky Plunge," *The Wall Street Journal,* 5 October 1989, p. A12.

p. 128 . . . might compromise its image as a high-end . . .

See "Amana Microwave Ovens," Harvard Business School case 9–579–182, revised July 1984. Professor Robert Buzzell was also very helpful in describing the industry dynamics of this time.

p. 128 . . . "when the pack thins out . . . "

Words of Don R. Cavalier, president of the marketing and sales division of Litton Microwave Cooking Products, as quoted in "Confident Execs Plan for Market Domination," *HFD,* 18 December 1978, p. 134.

p. 128 . . . positioning the machine as a *complete* cooking device.

See "Litton Microwave Cooking Products (C)," Harvard Business School case 9–477–085, p. 3.

p. 129 . . . *Mart,* a trade publication, chided . . .

Quoted in "Note on the Microwave Oven Industry," Harvard Business School case 9–579–185.

p. 129 . . . the *Wall Street Journal* complained . . .

See David M. Elsner, "Microwave Ovens Prove Hot Sellers Despite Recession," *The Wall Street Journal,* 22 April 1979, p. 31.

p. 129 . . . a similar theme was sounded by the publication *Merchandising Week.*

See *Merchandising Week,* September 1983, and *Merchandising Week,* March 1983.

p. 129 . . . the end of 1986, *Consumer Reports* noted . . .

See "Microwave Ovens," *Consumer Reports,* November 1986, p. 708.

p. 129 . . . like General Electric's new Spacemaker line . . .

See "General Electric Microwave Ovens," Harvard Business School case 9–579–184, revised July 1984.

p. 130 . . . syndicated real estate deals to the Japanese market . . .

Based on an interview with an investment banker serving the Japanese market.

p. 130 . . . when it introduced the 1988 Allanté . . .

See Keller, *Rude Awakening,* p. 217.

p. 131 . . . "Having sampled the 1990 model . . .

See John R. White, "Of improvements real, improvements imagined," *The Boston Globe,* 10 December 1989, p. A55.

p. 132 . . . "sweet and cold" rather than "acrid and hot."
See N. R. Kleinfield, "A Cold War Over Coffee," *The New York Times*, 29 October 1989, pp. F1, F11; also Michael J. McCarthy, "Test Shows That Pepsi's Rival to Coffee Hasn't Become Most People's Cup of Tea," *The Wall Street Journal*, 30 March 1990, pp. B1, B6.

p. 133 As one Easy Spirit convert explained . . .
See Elizabeth Bradburn and Annetta Miller, "Take a Hike, Cruel Shoes," *Newsweek*, 14 May 1990, p. 48.

p. 133 . . . U.S. Shoe's performance in some other areas . . .
See James S. Hirsch, "Questions About U.S. Shoe Corp. Continue to Mount," *The Wall Street Journal*, 5 April 1990, p. A6.

p. 133 . . . with a 200 percent growth rate for the two years after its introduction . . .
See Bradburn and Miller, "Take a Hike," p. 48.

p. 134 Tambrands, for example, was surprised at college students' . . .
See Suzanne Alexander, "Marketers Find College Crowd a Tough Test," *The Wall Street Journal*, 16 April 1990, p. B1.

p. 134 . . . that developed a better bug spray.
See Shanklin, *Six Timeless Marketing Blunders*, p. 131.

p. 135 . . . the effects of odors on consumers' attitudes on spending . . .
See Alecia Swasy, "Sellers May Find Scents Make Sense," *The Wall Street Journal*, 7 August 1990, p. B1.

p. 135 . . . "Domestic firms can do a superior job . . . "
See "Can Japanese Makers Take the Heat?," *HFD*, 29 March 1982, p. 32.

p. 136 . . . Nissan Motor Corporation took this approach one step further.
See Michael Lev, "Nissan Sued by U.S. Couple; Was Boarder Really a Spy?," *The New York Times*, 9 December 1989, p. 11.

p. 136 . . . as GTE Corp. found.
See Amanda Bennett and Carol Hymowitz, "For Customers, More Than Lip Service?," *The Wall Street Journal*, 6 October 1989, p. B1.

p. 138 . . . some have chosen to focus more on "designer names . . ."
See Francine Schwadel, "Complaints Rise About Clothing Quality," *The Wall Street Journal*, 27 June 1989, p. 15.

p. 138 When designer apparel is exported to Japan . . .
See Teri Agins and Yumiko Ono, "Japanese Market Lures,

Vexes Retailers," *The Wall Street Journal*, 29 May 1990, pp. B1, B6.

p. 138 . . . rejecting one such item because the stitching holes . . .
See Yumiko Ono, "Designers Cater to Japan's Love of Logos," *The Wall Street Journal*, 29 May 1990, p. B1.

p. 141 . . . classics in misunderstanding the consumer's trade offs: the IBM PCjr.
See Lele, *The Customer is Key*, pp. 69, 112.

p. 141 Andre Heiniger, managing director of Rolex . . .
See Shanklin, *Six Timeless Marketing Blunders*, p. 34.

Chapter 6: We Know How to Make a Buck

p. 147 . . . two employees of a fledgling company . . .
For the details of the Model 95 introduction, see Wensberg, *Land's Polaroid.*

p. 147 . . . another memorable product launch, this time for Spectra . . .
See Nicolas D. Kristof, "Polaroid Bets on New Camera; More Affluent Buyer Sought," *The New York Times*, 3 April 1986, p. D1.

p. 147 . . . with great panache, yet fell short of expectations.
See Keith H. Hammonds, "Polaroid's Spectra May Be Losing its Flash," *Business Week*, 29 June 1987, pp. 31–32. According to this article, Polaroid had planned to sell 800,000 Spectras in the camera's first year, but sold only 500,000 to 600,000, and sales were down 50 percent the following year.

p. 148 . . . the situation with Spectra was very different.
The materials in this chapter on Polaroid's Spectra come from Kristof, "Polaroid Bets on New Camera; More Affluent Buyer Sought;" Gail Bronson, "Watching the wrong birdie," *Forbes*, 28 April 1986, pp. 96, 100; Stan Grossfield, "Polaroid takes another shot at instant success," *The Boston Globe*, 3 April 1986, p. 61ff; and Hammonds, "Polaroid's Spectra May Be Losing its Flash."

p. 150 Cuisinart was blinded by this kind of pride . . . .
See N. R. Kleinfield, "How Cuisinart Lost Its Edge," *The New York Times Magazine*, 15 April 1990, pp. 46ff.

p. 151 . . . how the United States Time company unseated . . .
See Lele, *The Customer is Key*, pp. 206–207.

p. 152 . . . a few of Schnaars's examples . . .

For more details on the cool top range, quadraphonic sound systems, and videotex examples, see Schnaars, *Megamistakes.* Details on the "cool top" example are contained on pp. 39–40; on quadraphonic stereo, on p. 79; and on videotex, on pp. 55–56. The comment on videotex, as quoted in Schnaars, comes from Andrew Pollack, "Ruling May Not Aid Videotex," *The New York Times*, 15 September 1987, pp. D1, D6.

In the 1990s, products like Prodigy may fare differently, however, given a target market composed of people that already have personal computers in their homes.

p. 154 The vodka is Tanqueray Sterling . . .

See Joanne Lipman, "Tanqueray's Importer Will Test Brand's Appeal in Vodka Market," *The Wall Street Journal*, 16 August 1989, p. B5.

p. 155 . . . LP records accounted for less than 4 percent . . .

See Andrew Pollack, "Recording Enters a New Era, And You Can't Find It on LP," *The New York Times*, 1 April 1990, pp. 1, 24. The statistic on the decline of LP records cited in this article came from the Recording Industry Association of America; even taking out tape cassettes, by 1989, CDs were outselling LPs 6 to 1.

p. 155 . . . if he had listened to the experts, Sontheimer would have given up . . .

For the details on Cuisinart's early history, see Kleinfield, "How Cuisinart Lost."

p. 157 . . . when in 1981 it introduced the videodisc player in competition with . . .

See "Anatomy of RCA's Videodisc Failure," *Business Week*, 23 April 1984, pp. 89–90.

p. 159 . . . Porsche rolled back its prices . . .

See Thomas F. O'Boyle, "Porsche Succeeds in Revving Up U.S. Sales By Throttling Down Prices of Some Cars," *The Wall Street Journal*, 3 July 1989, p. 9.

p. 162 . . . one respondent to a 1988 survey by the magazaine *Global Investor* . . .

See *Global Investor*, May 1988, p. 7.

p. 162 . . . such customers may nevertheless stay with their current vendors . . .

That unhappy customers stay with current vendors when they have no better alternatives is not to say that having unhappy customers is a sustainable situation; obviously, as soon as there are competitors who offer a better deal, such customers will switch. But the point remains that customer satisfaction, in and of itself, is not as important as being able to offer a better deal than the competition can, and doing so on an ongoing basis.

p. 163 ... Bristol-Myers found this in 1975 ...

See Reis and Trout, *Marketing Warfare*; p. 62–64, 70; interview with a participant.

p. 167 Direct Tire, a Watertown, Massachusetts, enterprise ...

For more details, see Paul R. Brown, "The Real Cost of Customer Service," *Inc.,* September 1990, pp. 48ff.

p. 167 ... creativity guru Roger von Oech tells the story ...

See Roger von Oech, *A Whack on the Side of the Head,* Warner Books, New York, 1983, p. 105.

p. 167 ... Magaziner's analysis of GE's microwave oven business ...

See Magaziner, "Fast Heat."

p. 168 Parkinson's inspiration for his law ...

See Peter Brimelow, "How do you cure injelitance?," *Forbes,* 7 August 1989, p. 42.

p. 170 Jan Carlzon did as part of his turnaround of SAS ...

See Carlzon, *Moments of Truth,* p. 24.

p. 170 Leo McKernan did as part of his turnaround of Clark Equipment ...

See Brian Dumaine, "The New Turnaround Champs," *Fortune,* 16 July 1990, p. 42.

p. 170 Larry Bartlett did as part of his turnaround of Lube 'n Go ...

See Bruce G. Posner, "Squeeze Play," *Inc.,* July 1990, p. 69.

p. 171 ... Schlitz Brewing Company, holder of the number two share position ...

See Nash and Zullo, *The Mis-Fortune 500,* p. 10; also interview with a former distribution supervisor.

Chapter 7: We Understand What Our People Want

p. 177 ... start over again at the bottom of the ladder.

According to the rules in the industry, a pilot that went

to another airline started at the bottom of the seniority ladder. See Aaron Bernstein, *Grounded*, Simon & Schuster, New York, 1990, p. 18.

p. 177 . . . With the Eastern machinists on strike, Lorenzo faced . . .
The contract, the video, and the pilots' reactions are discussed in Bernstein, *Grounded*, p. 162.

p. 178 . . . a company spokesman dismissed the concern with the comment . . .
Quoted in Diana Solis and Jose de Cordoba, "Eastern Strike Bares Long-Festering Anger Over Sense of Betrayal," *The Wall Street Journal*, 17 March 1989, pp. A1, A12.

p. 178 . . . a 23-year veteran of the company, explained his ballot . . .
Quoted in Solis and de Cordoba, "Eastern Strike."

p. 178 "Fancy what a game of chess would be . . . "
This quote is from George Eliot's novel *Felix Holt,* (first published in 1866).

p. 180 . . . the recent experience of Levi Strauss in Hungary.
See Philip Revzin, "Ventures in Hungary Test Theory That West Can Uplift East Bloc," *The Wall Street Journal*, 5 April 1990, pp. A1, A14.

p. 180 . . . might side with Frederick Taylor . . .
Quoted in Pascale, *Managing on the Edge*, p. 102.

p. 180 . . . the recent experience at GM's Flint, Michigan, plant . . .
See Gregory A. Patterson, "UAW and Big Three Face Mutual Mistrust As Auto Talks Heat Up," *The Wall Street Journal*, 29 August 1990, p. A1.

p. 181 . . . point to the dramatic turnaround at SAS . . .
See Carlzon, *Moments of Truth*.

p. 181 . . . source of data comes from Daniel Yankelovich . . .
All of the Yankelovich data cited in this chapter come from Daniel Yankelovich, Hans Zetterberg, Burkhard Strumpel, Michael Shanks, John Immerwahr, Elisabeth Noelle-Neumann, Tamotsu Sengoku, and Ephraim Yuchtman-Yaar, *The World at Work: An International Report on Jobs, Productivity, and Human Values,* Octagon Books, New York, 1985. The data on the U.S. come from research done by Yankelovich and Immerwahr.

p. 183 . . . a company we'll call Spaulding Technologies . . .
Fictitious name and disguised industry and company details.

p. 187 Yankelovich and his colleague John Immerwahr tested . . .

The data in Table 7-1 were constructed as follows—"would contribute to motivation to work harder" includes Yankelovich's categories of "would work harder for" and "both" (i.e., both "work harder for" and "makes job more agreeable"); "makes job more agreeable" includes only Yankelovich's category of "makes job more agreeable." The data come from Yankelovich et al., *The World at Work*.

p. 192 . . . as Atsushi Kageyama, president . . .

See Atsushi Kageyama, "Looking for the Real Thing in Sony," *The Wall Street Journal*, 2 October 1989.

p. 192 . . . American workers in Mazda's Flat Rock, Michigan, plant . . .

See Joseph J. Fucini and Suzy Fucini, *Working for the Japanese: Inside Mazda's American Auto Plant*, The Free Press, New York, 1990, p. 104.

p. 193 This apparently happened at Value Line, Inc. . . .

See George Anders, "Value Line Inc. Is Hurt By Low Morale, Slide in Interest in Stocks, *The Wall Street Journal*, 15 April 1989.

p. 195 . . . the managers of one of GE's businesses got seven *daily* reports . . .

See Stratford P. Sherman, "The Mind of Jack Welch," *Fortune*, 27 March 1989.

p. 195 . . . conducted by Ellen Langer and two colleagues . . .

See E. Langer, A. Blank, and B. Chanowitz, "The Mindlessness of Ostensibly Thoughtful Action," *Journal of Personality and Social Psychology*, vol. 36, 1978, pp. 635–642. Langer's work on mindlessness and mindfulness are more fully described in Ellen J. Langer, *Mindfulness*, Addison-Wesley Publishing Company, Reading MA, 1989, p. 18.

Chapter 8: Our People Know What To Do

p. 205 . . . published the following overall comparison . . .

See Jack Thomas, "Four Seasons vs the Ritz," *The Boston Globe*, 2 March 1989, p. 77, 79.

p. 208 . . . considerable evidence that a hundred decisions a day . . .

The three studies used to illustrate this point—the two CEO

studies done by Mintzberg and Choron, and the foreman study done by Guest—are reported in Henry Mintzberg's book, *The Nature of Managerial Work*, Harper and Row, New York, 1973. The Guest study was originally published in 1956 as "Of Time and the Foreman," *Personnel*, vol. 32, 1956, pp. 478–486.

p. 209   Elliott Jaques would argue that they are.

See Elliott Jaques, *A General Theory of Bureaucracy*, Heinemann, London, 1976, p. 109; and Elliott Jaques, *Requisite Organization*, Cason Hall, Arlington VA, 1989, p. 36. Those seeking a shortcut to Jaques' work might refer to John S. Evans, *The Management of Human Capacity*, MCB Publications, Bradford, West Yorkshire, 1978.

p. 211   ... "SAS is 'created' 50 million times a year ..."

See Carlzon, *Moments of Truth*, p. 3.

p. 212   ... a survey conducted for The *Wall Street Journal* ...

See Francine Schwadel, "Shoppers' Blues: The Thrill is Gone," *The Wall Street Journal*, 13 October 1989, pp. B1-B2.

p. 212   ... are the product of outright sabotage as when ...

See Nash and Zullo, *The Mis-Fortune 500*, pp.130–131.

p. 214   In the Yankelovich and Immerwahr study ...

See Yankelovich et al., *The World of Work*.

p. 214   ... in terms of influence rather than control.

For a fuller treatment of this issue, see Allan R. Cohen and David L. Bradford, *Influence Without Authority*, John Wiley & Sons, New York, 1990.

p. 215   ... as former British Prime Minister Margaret Thatcher once advised ...

Quoted in *The London Sunday Times*, 18 March 1990, p. 1.

p. 217   *The Best Hospitals in America* listed the BI ...

See Linda Sunshine and John W. Wright, *The Best Hospitals in America*, Henry Holt and Company, New York, 1987; the figure of 6,500 short-stay hospitals comes from the total of 5,000 accredited by the Joint Commission on Accreditation of Hospitals plus an additional 1,500 that do not have JCAH accreditation.

p. 217   *Healthcare Forum Journal* counted the BI ...

See J. Daniel Beckham, "Winners: Strategies of ten of America's most successful hospitals," *Health Forum Journal*, November/December 1989, pp. 17–23.

p. 217 *Business Week* rated the BI . . .

    See John A. Byrne, "Profiting From the Nonprofits: Much Can Be Learned From Some of the Best-Run Organizations Around," *Business Week*, 26 March 1990, pp. 66ff.

p. 217 *The Service Edge: 101 Companies* . . .

    See Ron Zemke, *The Service Edge: 101 Companies that Profit from Customer Care*, New American Library, New York, 1989, p. 149.

p. 218 . . . Harvard researcher and Harmon Fellow Elizabeth Glaser.

    This research is published here for the first time. It was undertaken by Elizabeth Glaser, and I supervised and participated in the research effort. The agreement Glaser and I reached with the Beth Israel Hospital was that we would have unrestricted access to the hospital and its personnel, and that the results could be made public, warts and all. The only restriction was that patient care would not be impaired in any way.

    As a brief history, my involvement with this research began with a telephone call from Glaser, who was then the 1988–89 Harman Fellow for Public Policy, Technology and Human Development at Harvard University, and whose proposed research was on service quality. But Glaser had encountered an important problem: as she investigated possible sites for the field portion of her research, she found that the companies with the best reputations had better press than results. Her problem: to find a site where the service delivered was actually good enough to warrant further research without reinvestigating the handful of companies that are always held out as models of good service.

    Based on the experience of several people I knew who had been patients, I suggested that Glaser look at the BI as a potential research site. At that time, I knew little more about the hospital than its reputation, and Glaser had no information, so Glaser and I were able to formulate the hypotheses we wanted to test without many preconceived notions. The results were a surprise to both of us, but especially to Glaser, who began her observations with the point of view of a confirmed skeptic.

    We are both indebted to Professors Robert Eccles and Nithin Nohria of Harvard Business School, who helped us put together the research design for this project. We are also

255

indebted to Mitch Rabkin who gave us free rein of the hospital with no conditions on how we reported what we found, except that we report honestly.

p. 222 ... findings of Harvard Business School professor John Kotter...

See John P. Kotter, *The Leadership Factor,* The Free Press, New York, 1988.

p. 224 Federal Express, for example, has developed detailed... See Zemke, *The Service Edge.*

p. 225 Many "Nordies" are enthusiastic about their jobs ...

See Francine Schwadel, "Nordstrom's Push East Will Test Its Renown for the Best in Service," *The Wall Street Journal,* 1 August 1989, pp. A1, A4.

INDEX

Matsushita
and microwave ovens, 123
Mazda, 192
McColough, Peter
chairman of Xerox, 22, 23
McCune, William J.
and marketing of Polaroid
Spectra, 148
McGuffey's Restaurant
founding of, 60–62
McIlhenny Company, 107
McKernan, Leo
and costs at Clark Equipment,
170
McNamara, Robert, 107
Medawar, P.B.
on rejection of new ideas, 43
Mercedes 560L
competition for Cadillac Allanté,
130–31
Mercury Sable, 24
Merrill Lynch
downsizing of, 37–38
Microwave ovens, 30
consumer perception of, 127–29
cost of manufacturing in U.S.
and Korea, 167–68
marketing of, 135–36
See also Amana; General Electric;
Litton; Panasonic; Raytheon;
Samsung; Sharp
Miller, Herman
and the Scanlon plan, 197
MiniScribe
and measures taken to reach
sales goals, 97–98
history of, 99–101
Mintzberg, Henry, 208, 218
Modern Photography, 59
and the Polaroid Spectra, 149
Morimoto, Takahashi
and Nissan market research, 136
Morita, Akio
as chairman of Sony, 27
Morse, Peter
and acquisition of FAO Schwartz,
116
Morton Thiokol, 47, 62–63
"Moving Targets" test, 114

NASA
and Challenger disaster, 47
and investigation of Challenger
disaster, 62–63
solid rocket booster problems, 76
National Steel, 38
Nelson, Wayne
and Tylenol, 165
Nissan Motor Company
and failure of early Datsuns, 51
five-year plan to revitalize
company, 39–40
and innovative market research,
136
and name of Datsun 240 Z, 3
need for expansion beyond
Japan, 54
Nordstrom's
and customer service, 55
and employee satisfaction,
224–25
Norris, William C.
chairman of Control Data
Corporation, 27
Northwest Airlines
advertising campaign of, 5–6
NYNEX
and the videotex industry, 153

Oil Embargo of 1973
and effect on automobile size,
51–52
OSKAR
Sunbeam small food processor,
150–51
Overhead cost
as part of pricing considerations,
167–68

Panasonic
and Japanese management style,
192
and microwave ovens, 123
PARC (Palo Alto Research Center)
and Xerox development of
personal computer, 22–23
Parkinson's Law, 168
Penalties
for failures, 10